Cat In The Pulpit

by
Lois Sink

(Devotions for Cat Lovers)

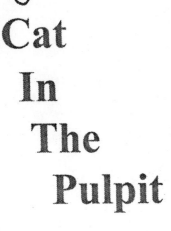

To Nancy,
From one cat lover
to another who met in
the Orlando, FL airport!
Lois Sink

xulon PRESS

Cat in the Pulpit
by Lois Sink

Printed in the United States of America

Library of Congress Control Number: 2003100862
ISBN 1-591604-70-2

You may contact the author by E-Mail at *sink@buffnet.net* or write her at 6449 Aiken Rd., Lockport, NY 14094-9646.

Xulon Press
www.xulonpress.com

To order additional copies, call 1-866-909-BOOK (2665).

Dedi "cat" ion

This book is lovingly dedi"cat"ed to Carl B. and Willetta Swanson. Ben and Willie were my landlord and his wife at Ashville, New York where the incidents recorded in this book occurred. They were also Fluffy's second parents, and she had the run of their first-floor apartment even though her main home was with me on the second floor.

Grateful thanks are due to my sister, Ruth K. Allison, who willingly took time from her busy schedule to edit the following pages. Ruth is also the author of "Dear Tabby," which appears in the middle of the book. Thank you, Ruth. I love you.

I would be remiss if I did not express my gratitude to Barbara Sutryn not only for her gentle and kind encouragement of my endeavors but also for suggesting the title of this book, *Cat in the Pulpit.* Thanks, Barbara. How I appreciate your support.

A Cat Owner's Prayer

Because I'm only human,
it's sometimes hard to be
The wise, all-knowing creature
that my cat expects of me.
And so I pray for special help
to somehow understand
The subtle implications of
each proud meowed command.
Oh, let me not forget that chairs
were put on Earth to shred,
And what I like to call a lap
is actually a bed.
I know it's really lots to ask
but please, oh please, take pity,
And though I'm only human,
make me worthy of my Kitty!!!!

Anonymous

Preface

Let me introduce you to Fluffy—my adorable, long-haired, yellow-and-white feline companion. She is ten years old, and how I do "love" her! Life was quite boring before she came to live with me!

If it is true that each year of a cat's life is equal to seven human years, my kitty and I are the same age! However, neither of us is sensitive about revealing our age because we don't look or act as old as we are—although I will admit that a few arthritic joints discourage one of us (me) from cavorting around the house in pursuit of the other.

The many lessons I have learned from Fluffy have been fraught with spiritual overtones. I am constantly amazed by the unquestioning trust she displays as she permits me to hold her on her back the way one would cuddle a baby. It is a compliment, indeed, when a cat willingly submits to being held in such a fashion. When, however, the kitty sings, with closed and contented eyes, while being thus held—this is said to be the highest possible compliment a cat can pay to a human being. To my great delight, that is Fluffy's favorite way of being held! But as I gently rock her, I have to ask, "Should not I display the same degree of trust in my Heavenly Father?"

That spiritual lesson, and scores of others which Fluffy has taught me, will unfold in the following vignettes. My prayer is that all of you cat lovers will not only be entertained by these true incidents but will also find them an inspiration in your Christian walk.

I dread the day when Fluffy and I must be separated by the Grim Reaper. But as sad and difficult as it will be to say the final welfare, I do hope, for her sake, that she will be ushered through the catnip gates of "kitty heaven" to roam vast fields of clover BEFORE I am ushered through the pearly gates of Glory to walk on shining streets of gold in that very real, very wondrous, and eternal City "John saw coming down!"

Table of Contents

A Dual Citizenship

But our citizenship is in heaven. Philippians 3:20 (NIV)

Fluffy is a Canadian by birth. I never asked my friends who brought her across the border whether they had to "declare" her, pay import duty, or name her city of birth when going through customs. She had neither a visa nor a passport. She's never been issued a "green card" to live or work in this country; nor have I heard that she's limited to any particular number of years she may remain in the United States without losing her Canadian citizenship.

Fluffy has been a resident of our fair country for approximately nine years now, and not once has she returned to Canada for even so much as a "How-do-you-do" to her former owners. Wonder if there's such a thing as "common law" that would automatically establish permanent residency for her after a certain period of time?

Since immigration authorities have not contacted me regarding my "better half" nor charged me with harboring an illegal alien, I'm assuming that Fluffy is now a citizen of both the United States and Canada. One thing I've noticed, though, is that it matters not to her whether I'm displaying the grand old stars and stripes or flying a flag with a maple leaf!

It's not every cat that can boast of dual citizenship!

Father, I may be in this world, but I don't have to be of it! Although I thank You for the privilege of living in this great nation of ours that still offers many blessings and freedoms, I also thank You because I'm a citizen of a far better country called Heaven where mansions, joys untold, and pleasures forevermore await me.

A Mighty Hunter She

Watch out for Satan. . .He prowls around like a hungry, roaring lion, looking for some victim to tear apart.
I Peter 5:8 (TLB)

Although Fluffy basically is no hunter, she does enjoy stalking small prey, including chipmunks, now and then.

Recently when I jumped into the car to start my daily errands, I glanced at the nearby bird feeders and noticed her tense little body crouched in the tall grass beneath as she eyed some unsuspecting creature moving among the lilac trees. Ordinarily when she sees me outdoors, she leaves whatever she is doing and races over to be petted. This time, however, she didn't so much as twitch a whisker to acknowledge my presence.

I knew that in all probability she would never be able to capture her prey for lack of front claws. But I wondered if the poor creature she was just waiting to pounce on wasn't suffering a full-blown panic attack. After all, he didn't know how harmless she really was and saw her as a formidable life-threatening foe.

"Have fun, Fluffy," I whispered as I smiled to myself and backed out the drive.

Thank You, Father, for showing me so clearly in Your Word that although Satan is walking through this earth looking for whomever he can devour, he's only masquerading as a hungry roaring lion and has no more power over me than I allow him to have. Because of the blood of Christ and Your Word, I need not be afraid, knowing I have victory over the enemy even as I resist him in the precious name of Jesus.

A Trap of Her Own Making

Don't let me hear of your. . .
prying into other people's affairs.
I Peter 4:15 (TLB)

If Fluffy hadn't been prying into other people's affairs, namely, my landlord's garage, she wouldn't have gotten herself locked in for the night!

She had been gone for several hours. I thought nothing about it as we have approximately a quarter of an acre where she roams at will and smugly remains as Top Cat on the hill. Add to that the neighbor's fair-sized property, two hillsides and no-man's land that adjoins the cemetery, and she could have been anywhere. I really wasn't too concerned for I knew she'd come home for supper—but she didn't.

I certainly got my exercise walking that evening. So did Ben and Willie, my landlord and his wife, as well as the neighbors. After all, Fluffy belongs to everybody on the hilltop—she just happens to make my apartment her headquarters. Eventually the others tired of the hunt; but a mother, of course, will never give up hope that her wandering lost child will be found.

All of us, of course, had been calling Fluffy by name as we looked every place we could think of. But there was no welcoming reply to our urgent summons. As dusk wrapped its delicate arms around the hilltop, bathing it in soft quietness, I uttered a low moan of sheer distress, "Fluffy, Fluffy, where, oh, where are you?" To my utter astonishment, I heard plaintive, repeated "meows." I pricked up my ears and called again. By now the meows were getting louder and more frantic, and I soon traced them to Ben's locked garage.

Ben, you understand, is a professional painter and has all kinds of paint cans and tools stored in his garage, together with his pickup truck, a snow blower, a riding lawn mower, garden plows, ladders, and a host of other good things—a perfect place for a cat to snoop, then curl up and take a nap!

Once I located Fluffy's hideaway, it was just a minute or two until Ben released her from her prison—a prison of her own making, a prison that was the direct result of her snooping and prying into someone else's personal affairs.

'Nuf said?

Lord, why is it that it's such a temptation to snoop into the affairs of others even though I know their private lives are none of my business? Somehow I seem to think I'm doing my "religious duty" when I engage in such despicable conduct and even try to offer unasked-for advice. I don't like the term "busybody," Lord, but there's no other word that adequately describes such actions, and I know from experience that I often fall into a trap of my own making because I engage in such practice. Forgive me, I pray, and help me, from this day forward, to keep my eyes on You and spend my efforts in keeping my own house in order.

Alert and Watching

Watch and pray, that ye enter not into temptation.
Matthew 26:41 (KJV)

I never cease to marvel how Fluffy appears to be asleep when, in reality, she is only dozing and is on automatic pilot. She often wakes up with a start and focuses on a minute insect flying across the room. In fact, the flying gnat is so small I can't even find it, not even with my new trifocals. My main concern, however, is that she's spied a spider—the one thing I'm deathly afraid of! I always keep several cans of spray repellent in strategic spots to protect myself from possible attacks.

Other times Fluffy's sensitive ears detect a faint noise floating through the door from the nearby highway. Then she jumps to her feet with a start.

Do cats dream, I wonder? Occasionally she'll get awake from what appears to be a deep sleep, bound off my lap, run into the next room and peer intently around the corner. *Is there really something there? Or has she had a nightmare?* I question. *Could it be just nerves? Or do cats even have nerves? Could the vet give me nerve pills for her?*

I may never get answers to my questions. But this one

thing I know—Fluffy is alert and sensitive to her surroundings.

Loving Father, may I always be as alert and sensitive to my surroundings as Fluffy is to hers. May I be especially alert when it comes to hearing Your voice. Help me when temptations come upon me unawares, to recognize Satan's tactics and to resist him with the name of Jesus, the Blood of Christ, and the Word of God.

All on the Altar

...(T)heir sacrifices will be accepted on My altar.
Isaiah 56:7 (Amp.)

Fluffy had been sick for more than eight weeks, and no one knew what was wrong. Multiple trips to the vet were fruitless. Medicine gave only a temporary reprieve. First I thought she might have had an encounter with a stray tom cat that had been slinking behind the garage for several days. Then I decided it was the new brand of cat food she had been eating. I even wrote to the company and, at their request, sent them the unopened cans to be analyzed when they offered to reimburse me for doctor and hospital expenses if, indeed, the food had been tainted and caused her unexplained illness. But nothing was wrong with the cat food, they reported. *Perhaps she has tried to eat the new house plant I just purchased and set on the front porch,* I reasoned. Maybe it was a member of the Dieffenbachia family, a genus that can be fatal to cats. I gave the plant to a friend who had no pets.

Because of the expense, and because the results were only temporary, I discontinued Fluffy's dreaded trips to the vet. Her bouts with illness lasted three days whether or not she received medication. The only thing the vet did that I couldn't do was give her shots of water to ward off dehydration. She was listless; she wouldn't eat; she cried when I picked her up. If she could only have talked and told me what was wrong, I might have been able to cope. But after two months, I, too, got sick—sick from worry. My blood pressure soared as I could think of nothing else. I was apprehensive and would sleep the morning away so I wouldn't have to get up and face another day, not knowing what to do with my precious furry companion. She wasn't sick enough to justify "putting her away," yet it would have been a relief not to see her mope around while I was helpless to ease her pain.

Finally, in desperation, I offered a prayer that nearly tore my heart out. I thanked the Lord for giving me Fluffy all these years and then told Him that I put her in His hands completely as I realized He knew what was best for both of us. My only request was that His will be done, and prayed that if it was time to part with her, He would take her quickly and easily as well as see me through the emotional trauma that I knew would follow. "Live or die, she's yours, Lord," I concluded my prayer.

"You did the right thing," a friend in whom I confided told me, "to lay her on the altar."

So that was the meaning of that old hymn that asks, "Is your all on the altar?" I had never fully understood it before, but now it made perfect sense!

Yes, Fluffy recovered and is as good as new these days!

Thank You, Father, for the blessings of peace and sweet rest that You bestow upon Your children when we put everything into Your capable hands and let You control all the details of our lives. Thank You, too, that nothing is too small nor insignificant to bring to You—even the welfare of pets.

Answer Me!

Speak, Lord; for thy servant heareth.
I Samuel 3:9 (KJV)

Although Fluffy has numerous hiding places throughout the house, I know her favorite haunts and can usually find her—unless I leave both the attic door and the outside door open at the same time. Then it's anybody's guess where she might be.

Once in a while, though, she'll discover a new hiding place and forget to show me where it is. On those rare occasions, however, I walk from room to room calling, "Fluffy, where are you?" If that is unsuccessful—and it usually is—I issue an ultimatum in a much sterner tone of voice: "Answer me, Fluffy, answer me!" The longer it takes her to heed my command—and she does love to play "possum"—the more adamant I become. Eventually she gets the message—loud and clear—and makes her appearance right behind me, looking up at me with the most innocent expression a cat could assume. Of course she always sneaks out of her secret hiding place after I've gone into another room, so I still don't know where she's been hanging out!

All I can say is, I'm glad the boy Samuel, in the Old

Testament account, answered the Lord more quickly than Fluffy answers my summons!

Father, I confess that many are the times I fail to answer Your loving voice because I have an idea of what You might want, and it isn't exactly what I want to hear! Forgive me, Lord, and help me to be quick to respond to Your call, thereby keeping the lines of communication open between us.

Battle Scars

...(T)hey shall fight, because the Lord is with them.
Zechariah 10:5 (KJV)

In the flesh, it is I, not Fluffy, who wears the battle scars—battle scars inflicted by my sweet little companion! To begin with, Fluffy's not a small cat; she also has long hair (whence her name) which makes her appear larger yet. Friends tell me I've taught her to play rough—so I guess it's my own fault I sport a few scars.

You see, Fluffy has no front claws. That was not my choice, for I would never feel comfortable depriving an animal of its natural means of climbing or protecting itself. (On occasion, I have known her to do a limited amount of climbing, although I've never understood how she manages it!) But Fluffy fares quite well without front claws for she has good, sharp teeth which she doesn't hesitate to use in a deadly, slashing motion when I play with her too roughly. Her accompanying hiss plainly says, "This is my absolute final warning before I shred you to ribbons." Other times she will brace her hind feet—which do have claws—against my hand or arm and give a leap into space that rivals a blast-off from Cape Canaveral. Blood spurts from my arm like sparks from a launching pad.

Sometimes it seems I spend as much money on band-aids—all sizes, all shapes—as I do on cat food! People didn't call me "Red' for nothing when I was a kid; and all the rest of you erstwhile redheads know how red hair and fair skin seem to complement each other! So the majority of these bites and scratches that Fluffy so lovingly delivers (yes, I'm being sarcastic!) leave permanent scars on my tender flesh. Of course, if I would learn to leave them alone and let Mother Nature take care of healing them by herself, I'm sure the number of scars would decrease!

Oh, well—I guess scars are part of any battle, whether in play, in real life or in spiritual matters. At least I'll never be able to forget my pet, for I'll carry scars in loving memory of Fluffy forever.

Spiritually speaking, I'm reminded of a verse from an old Herbert Buffum gospel song which I haven't seen in print for years. It says, in part:

I would be among that number
who could show some battle scars,
Telling how they fought for Jesus
and received the crown and stars.

Father, when spiritual battles rage fast and furious, help me remember that I am not fighting in my own strength but in the might and power of the Lord Jesus Christ Who bore the scars of Calvary for me. And may I carry with pride and dignity any scars that I am called upon to bear for You.

Bedfellows

...(Y)ou are my friends.
John 15:15 (TLB)

Because I'm single, I've always slept alone. On the few occasions when I visit, travel, etc., and have to bunk with another person, I get very little sleep. I'm just used to having the bed to myself—that's probably why I've learned to spread out over the entire bed, kick off the blankets when I'm hot, and tuck them all around myself when I'm cold! Good thing marriage doesn't loom in the foreseeable future for me, for I'm sure my spouse would find it difficult to put up with my nighttime antics.

Having Fluffy for a bedfellow, however, is a different story. Not only does she not make too many demands space wise, but she also doesn't seem to care how much I "hog" the covers.

She does have her nightly routine, though, as I suppose all intelligent people and animals do. First of all, we play the game of "Catch" to see whether I'm going to carry her to bed or whether she's going to retire on her own when she gets good and ready. (She's taught me that cats usually do whatever they want to do whenever they want to do it!) It's a 50/50 no-win situation. Regardless of how she gets there, she trots to the head of the bed, jumps onto the night stand in front of the window and gazes out upon our large back yard. Once satisfied that the outside world is under control, she steps back onto the bed and nuzzles her wet nose under the blankets for a ten or fifteen-minute snuggle in the crook of my arm while she sings a bedtime lullaby to me. Sleepy at last, she makes her way to the foot of the bed which is the last I hear of her until the middle of the night. And if I'm in a deep sleep, I really don't hear her even then. I just roll over and there she is, all curled up on the pillow beside me!

I'd say we were pretty good friends, now, wouldn't you, for her to be able to take all those liberties in my bed?

Father, how wonderful to be called Your friend and to know that You are a Friend of mine, a Friend Who sticks closer than a brother. Thank You for the privilege of hiding in You even as Fluffy hides under the blankets with me. Thank You for the comfort and rest I find in the shelter and protection of Your mighty arms of love.

Bird Watching

...God, who richly provides us
with everything for our enjoyment.
I Timothy 6:17 (NIV)

Because Fluffy seldom gets out of the house during our long New York winters, I felt, one year, that it was my duty as a doting parent to provide her with entertainment. After all, there has to be more to life than sleeping twenty-four hours a day even if one is a cat. So I hung bird feeders all along the front porch of our second-story apartment, then raised the Venetian blinds so she could watch the ensuing action to her heart's content as birds of all descriptions quickly found a "birdie smorgasbord." All Fluffy had to do was jump on the back of the davenport in front of one window, or perch atop the easy chair at the other window. Even when she sat on my lap in the La-Z-Boy half way across the room, she had a clear vision of the bird feeders—not one, or two, or even three, but seven of them!

That winter I went through two 50-lb. bags of sunflower seeds as well as several smaller bags of mixed seed, then wondered why I suddenly had to make an appointment to see the chiropractor after I carried those bags from the car to my upstairs attic! Ben, my landlord, claimed that his bird-feeding business in the back yard fell off by at least sixty percent. Even the new neighbors complained because they had no birds at all visiting the one lone feeder just outside their kitchen window where they had looked forward to bird watching during the cold months of winter!

Those seven bird feeders, though, kept Fluffy occupied a good share of the time—until she learned she couldn't capture any of her little feathered friends. Occasionally, when a sparrow or purple finch would hop to the inside of the porch to escape a vicious snow storm, she would attempt to dive through the window which reached from ceiling to the floor. Eventually she tired of all the fluttering and chirping of our hungry guests and did no more than flick a sleepy eye in their direction.

I, too, got tired of winter entertainment—tired of pulling on boots, gloves and other necessary cold-weather paraphernalia, tired of sweeping snow off the porch, and tired of refilling the feeders three or four times weekly. Tired, also, of dragging the vacuum sweeper all the way from the back attic to the living room to repair the damage of the snow and bird seed I tracked across the carpet every time I came in. Wearily I awaited the coming of Spring, but was dismayed to discover one glorious March day when the snow had melted that the porch floor was covered not only with discarded hulls of sunflower seeds, but also with mixed bird seed that our feathered friends had scattered far and wide. I must have swept up a good five pounds of uneaten seeds!

Thank goodness my landlord decided to build a new porch for me that summer, or I never would have gotten rid of the bird seed that had fallen into the cracks between the floor boards, refusing to yield to the ministrations of a broom! My bird feeders now sit, empty and forlorn, in the attic and I leave the bird feeding up to Ben and the neighbors. In the meantime, Fluffy is as content as ever without winter-time bird watching.

Father, thank You not only for supplying all of my needs, but also for giving me all things richly to enjoy. Truly You thought of so many things that make life pleasurable, especially in the realm of nature; and for this, I give You praise.

Can Opener Magic

I have learned by experience...
Genesis 30:27 (KJV)

It's all Willie's fault! Now I really do appreciate the fact that she and Ben live downstairs and am grateful that they take care of Fluffy whenever I'm on vacation or gone for a few days. But I'll never forget the first time I returned from a short trip.

It was late in the day when I got home to an empty refrigerator. Too exhausted to prepare a meal, I decided to content myself with a can of soup. At the first sound of the can opener, however, Fluffy came tearing into the kitchen, rubbing against my legs and meowing pathetically as though she hadn't had anything to eat the entire time I was away. I knew better than that! *But why did the can opener attract her?* I wondered. *She'd never paid any attention to it before!*

Not until the next day was the mystery solved. Apparently Ben and Willie use a lot of tuna fish—"people" tuna, of course. Rather than throw out the juice, Willie decided to add some water and see if Fluffy would drink it. Are you kidding me? She didn't drink it—she guzzled it like the town drunk imbibing a bottle of Jack Daniels!

Now I don't mind giving Fluffy the juice whenever I open a can of tuna. Nor do I mind Willie saving her tuna juice and giving it to Fluffy when she makes her daily trips downstairs. But feeding her tuna juice has had a detrimental side effect—she's learned from experience the magic of a can opener!

So beware of using an electric can opener if you ever visit me, for you'll immediately have a cat winding it's way around your legs, impeding your progress.

Well, I guess I shouldn't complain, for there are worse things than can openers she could learn about!

Father, although there are many things I've gleaned from life's varied experiences—some pleasant and some otherwise—the most important truth I've learned is that You love me and have a plan for my life. Thank You for the lessons You teach me daily. May I always be quick to learn what You desire to teach me, knowing that I can profit from all circumstances that confront me.

Cat Violence

The kingdom of heaven suffereth violence,
and the violent take it by force.
Matthew 11:12 (KJV)

Cats are sensitive creatures, easily hurt if one ignores them when they try to tell you about their needs and experiences. Fluffy is no exception.

Men are a favorite with Fluffy. This is especially obvious when Dan, whom I call my "adopted son," drops in. Was one of her previous owners male? I'll never know.

The last time Dan visited me was to help set up my new computer. How Fluffy cried for his attention from the moment he crossed the threshold. She continued her pathetic, yet demanding yowls and rubbed against his legs until he stopped his work and petted her to her heart's content. Then, and only then, was he able to concentrate on what, for us, was a far more important issue than Fluffy's feelings. Eventually satisfied with his attention, she curled up at his feet, and before long, my computer was up and running.

A few weeks later, when my girlfriend dropped in to learn about the wonders of E-mail and internet since she contemplated buying a computer, Fluffy became even more demanding than she had been with Dan. I had never seen her act this way with a woman. Perhaps she caught the doggie scent of Chief, Bernice's German Shepherd, but that is unlikely because Fluffy can't "stand" dogs! So why the ardent attraction? Somewhat absent mindedly, Bernice reached down to pet Fluffy while at the same time her focus was riveted to the computer monitor. It didn't take long for Fluff to realize that she was not receiving Bernice's undivided attention. And with one urgent screech of demanding protest, she bit Bernice's leg right through her clothing. On second thought, I wondered if she was displaying indignation over the fact that Bernice would actually invade our apartment with the scent of a dog on her clothes! Either way, I was both shocked and dismayed by such abhorrent conduct toward a guest!

My only consolation is that Fluffy has never repeated her bizarre behavior!

Heavenly Father, thank You that I can learn from Fluffy's actions, undesirable as they sometimes are. May I always be persistent not only in presenting my petitions before the throne of grace but also in fighting against the enemy of my soul, even to the point of spiritual violence, when necessary.

Caught Between a Rock and a Hard Place

...(T)his is the way, walk ye in it.
Isaiah 30:21 (KJV)

Fluffy was pacing throughout the apartment. Ere long I discovered the source of her restlessness—the neighbor's cat, Shoe, was sound asleep on our davenport. (Shoe got her name because as a kitten, she loved to play with an old shoe!) Fluffy hated other cats, both big and little. Shoe was no exception, even though she was a neighbor. Of course, she hadn't endeared herself to Fluffy by visiting us whenever she chose, without an invitation, at that! She also took advantage of our hospitality by eating Fluffy's expensive food that I purchased from the vet's.

On the day in question, Fluffy eventually went out to the den and curled up for her afternoon nap on the day bed. But that didn't solve the quandary of what I was to do with Shoe, a tiny little thing less than half the size of Fluffy. I liked her. She was very affectionate and I was honored to think she chose my apartment as her "second" home. Nevertheless, I was between a rock and a hard place, or perhaps it would be more nearly to correct to say I was between Shoe and Fluffy!

I mentally debated the pros and cons of my "sticky" situation and decided it would be wise to take Shoe downstairs and start her on her homeward journey. After all, it was a sunny day—it wasn't as though I were putting her out in a storm with no place to go! Gently I lifted her from her warm nest on the davenport, cuddling her as I did so. Her "motor" sounded like a buzz saw—until I got to the top of the stairs, that is. The moment Shoe caught sight of the stairs, she began crying and continued her pathetic mewls all the way downstairs as though I were physically abusing her! I felt like a first-class traitor! How can a cat that small make a human person as big as I am (no comments, please!) feel so low down, rotten dirty?

Securely closing all doors to circumvent a return visit, I retraced my steps, picked up Fluffy and began to cuddle her, thinking I could thus placate her hurt feelings. Nothing doing! She began to cry and didn't even want to be held! Seems all I had done was take the "rock" outside and left the "hard place" in my apartment.

Heavenly Father, many are the incidents of daily life in which I find myself caught between a rock and a hard place. How thankful I am that in those difficult periods of stress I can lift my heart to You for guidance and direction, knowing I will hear the sweet, gentle voice of Your Spirit telling me what to do, which way to go, and the best way to handle the situation.

Cat Trivia

FLUFFY EXPLAINS BODY LANGUAGE

"Body language tells cats a lot about their humans," declares Fluffy. "For example, if my human holds out her hand and wiggles her fingers, I know she is beckoning me to come to her. Or if she sits in her La-Z-Boy and pats her knees, she's summoning me to jump on her lap. Likewise, humans can understand cats by watching our ears, our eyes, and even our tails."

"When our ears are pointed straight up," she explains, "it's because we're happy campers. But if you see our ears flat against our heads, you can be sure that something is frightening us or making us angry. And when we get nervous about something, we'll point our ears backwards. On the other hand, if our ears are pointed slightly forward, we're alert to something we're not quite sure about."

"Whenever you see our eyes half closed," she continues, "there's nothing wrong with our eyes. Nor are we falling asleep. We're just letting you know we're contented. On the other hand, however, our eyes will be wide open and alert whenever we're playing. And if we get frightened, the pupils of our eyes will dilate."

"Our tails can tell you a lot about us, too," shares Fluffy. "When you see us carrying them high, we're just letting you know how happy we are to see you. And while we don't exactly wag our tails like a dog, we do give them a gentle switch now and then to indicate we're pleased. But be careful if you see us give a strong thrash of our tails, for that means we're irritated and upset about something."

"If you see us stretching our bodies, extending and retracting our claws slowly, that's a sign we're happy."

Chasing Enemies

Resist the devil, and he will flee from you.
James 4:7 (KJV)

Fluffy was resting on the cool cement of the downstairs back porch one early Spring day. The outside door was partially open in case she wanted to venture into the yard. The neighbors laughingly related the rest of the story to me.

They were looking out their kitchen window which faces our back door when they spied a black dog, many times larger than Fluffy (and she's not tiny by any means) nudge our back porch door enough to allow him to squeeze his bulky frame inside—but he never made it. They said he backed out faster than he meandered in, then turned around when he got at a safe distance only to see a large orange and white ball throttling toward him spitting and hissing for all she was worth. The overgrown canine took no chances. Tucking his tail beneath his legs, he fled for his life down over the hill. For some strange reason, he hasn't visited Fluffy since! In fact, he hasn't even dared return to the hilltop.

I can envision the headlines of the next day's "Cat and Dog Daily News": Orange and White Tornado Causes Black and White Mongrel to Flee for His Life.

Hm-m-m! Do I have that much courage?

When I asked Fluffy later how she felt about her accomplishment, she simply sighed, "It was good 'mews'!"

Lord, grant me a holy boldness in chasing my spiritual enemies whether they be fear, doubt, unbelief, or other besetting sins. You have told me in Your Word that I can do all things through Christ Who strengthens me. Help me to be strong, courageous, and aggressive toward the enemy. Remind me always that the battle is not mine alone as I have the Holy Spirit to empower me in all situations.

Chippy Chipmunk

(D)on't begin until you count the cost.
Luke 14:28 (TLB)

One beautiful August day, I spied Fluffy resting in the shade of the long, green turf at the edge of the hillside between our yard and the side road. The way she was sitting, spread eagle, with legs outstretched, and tummy flat on the grass, reminded me of a little red hen hovering over a nest of eggs, patiently waiting for them to hatch. She was so irresistible I had to pick her up with the intention of cuddling her and tickling her silky white belly. But when she uttered a sharp cry of pain, I jumped away in dismay. Cautiously I approached her again and timidly reached out to pet her. She cried only when I touched her stomach, I noticed. *What could be wrong?* I worried.

I let her rest a while in her cool grassy nest before carrying a plastic bowl of fresh water to her. Refreshed from her drink, she slowly began to walk around the yard but refused to allow me to pick her up. With a sigh of relief, I went back in the house, still pondering what could have happened. Before long she was none the worse as a result of whatever experience had befallen her.

Later that day, when I was taking the garbage to the compost pile at the rear of our lot and admiring the beauty of the newly-mown back yard, something white caught my eye. I stepped aside to investigate, and there, between the woodsy clumps of lilac bushes and wild roses were gobs and gobs of long, white kitty fur! *How? What? Why?* Questions flew through my mind faster than speeding bullets in war time. Forgetting my errand, I called Ben, my landlord, to come see this unusual phenomenon. As we speculated and pondered, contemplated and surmised, we eventually pieced together what must have happened to Fluffy earlier that day.

We have a horde of chipmunks on our premises who hang around to feed on the dainty morsels Ben puts out for the birds. Fluffy must have sneaked up on an unsuspecting chippy and actually caught him even though she has no front claws. Apparently the chippy put up a fight; and as Fluffy hung onto him, he clung to her like a baby opossum riding upside down on its mother's tummy. In the ensuing battle, the chipmunk evidently fought the only way he knew how: by pulling handfuls—I mean pawfuls—of hair from Fluffy's silky little underside before escaping. No wonder her tummy was sore when I tried to lift her!

Know what? Fluffy doesn't chase "chippies" any more. She's counted the cost and is now content to watch from afar!

Chasing chipmunks just isn't worth the pain.

Father, so many times I act and speak without thinking of the suffering and pain my words might cause a brother or a sister. Help me not to be rash in my speech but to let the words of my mouth, as well as the meditations of my heart, be acceptable in Your sight, O Lord, my God and my Savior.

Choir Director

He himself gives life and breath to everything.
Acts 17:25 (TLB)

Although I play many musical instruments, my specialty is the keyboard—both piano and organ. My fingers were too tender to build up the necessary callouses for playing the guitar and other stringed instruments. Actually, I did play both trombone and baritone for several years in the Salvation Army, but I really wasn't the "hottest thing" in the band! My problem, apparently, was faulty breathing technique. I had taken a few vocal lessons in my early teens, but oh, what trouble I had with one of my breathing exercises—learning to pant!

Then, in my mid-thirties, I was asked to attend a music camp as a theory instructor as well as accompanist for several choirs. When I discovered I had some free time, I enrolled in a vocal class hoping to learn correct breathing methods. How surprised I was to discover that a study of Fluffy's breathing patterns could show me the proper technique I needed—not only for singing but also for playing wind instruments!

When I returned home, I watched her carefully as her

soft, little diaphragm steadily expanded and contracted—in and out, in and out in perfect rhythm. Enlightenment suddenly flooded my mind. When I breathed, it was not "in and out" but "up and down" as I gulped for a deep breath while my shoulders rose and fell, rose and fell. But not once did Fluffy gasp or raise her shoulders in an effort to get her lungs full of air—a common error, I learned, that humans untrained in the art of correct breathing often make when trying to sing. For breathing incorrectly while the shoulders move up and down only constricts the diaphragm, making it more difficult to produce a rich and full melodic sound. At last I knew what my vocal teacher of long years ago was trying to demonstrate when she encouraged me in the art of "panting!" And once I learned to breathe properly, it improved not only my singing but also increased my ability in playing wind instruments.

How many times since then I've used Fluffy as an illustration when I, in turn, have had opportunity to share pointers with my fellow choir members. I guess she'll never know how influential she's been in teaching proper breathing techniques to aspiring vocalists, thereby improving the quality of our local church music, both vocal and instrumental!

Thank you, Fluffy. You're one great teacher!

Thank You, Father, for giving life and breath to me. May I improve my talents and use them for Your honor and glory in praising You and blessing my fellow worshipers through the ministry of music—music which flows from the great heart of God.

Contentment

I have learned the secret of contentment in every situation.
Philippians 4:12 (TLB)

My landlord, Ben, tells me that Fluffy's "my baby" (I already knew that!) because I hold her on her back like a mother holds a baby! Believe it or not—maybe I should try for a prominent place in Ripley's *Believe It Or Not*—Fluffy makes no objection to being held in this manner. In fact, she'll purr like a buzz saw. I wouldn't, however, advise anyone else to try holding her so intimately. Others have tried it, occasionally, but with vastly different results you don't even want to know about!

When you hold a cat on her back and she purrs, she is, indeed, paying you a high compliment. How I love to be complimented! If my fellow men won't compliment me, I know where to go to get all the compliments I need–I go to "my baby!" That's right, Ben—"my baby!" But the highest compliment of all, cat authorities say, is for a cat to purr and close her eyes while she's being held on her back. Why, Fluffy does that all the time, especially if I bury my face in the soft, white, silky hair of her tummy that curls so invitingly.

That's another thing that puzzles me. If I rub her tummy with my hands when she's on her back, she'll kick and bite until she draws blood. But never once has she shown anything but pure contentment when I nuzzle her underside with my face. Who taught her, I wonder, that my face and my hands are two different things? That it's OK to scratch hands but not faces? As I've said before, she's one smart cat—possibly the intelligence has rubbed off from association with her owner!

Also, Fluffy has learned to be content in whatsoever way she's being held—at least when I'm the one holding and cuddling her!

Dear Lord, may I, like Fluffy, learn to be content in whatsoever state I find myself, for I know that nothing happens to me without Your knowledge and Your approval. And when I encounter rough, difficult situations in my life, I know that even then You will cause all things to work for my good.

Demanding Little Rascal

Let us therefore come boldly unto the throne of grace.
Hebrews 4:16 (KJV)

How I dread taking Fluffy to the vet for her annual checkup, even though it's just a ten-minute drive. For starters, she hates riding in a car. Secondly, she detests a cat carrier even more. She begins her yearly journey with a few plaintive meows. By the time we reach the end of our driveway and negotiate the short side street to the main highway, her cries increase both in intensity and frequency. When that doesn't change the situation, she turns her frantic pleas into incessant, howling demands. By the time we reach our destination, she is grasping the bars of the carrier much like a monkey in the zoo while actually shaking the door as hard as she can. Thank goodness that door has a double fastener!

Submitting to the ministrations of the vet doesn't help her disposition any, and the trip home is an endurance test for me. Will I make it without my sanity taking flight? Or will she wear me down? When we return to the familiar home ground of our premises where I can safely open both the car door and cat carrier, she literally "flops" on the macadam drive utterly exhausted. If it weren't for the watchful eyes of the neighbors, I think I'd follow suit!

Only once did I take her with me on a short vacation—the longest two-hour trip I've ever taken in my entire life. I don't know what kept her from getting laryngitis. Do you have any idea what it's like to listen to the constant caterwauling of a feline for ninety long miles, demanding that the car be stopped, and stopped now? No more cozy vacations for two so far as I'm concerned!

Fluffy is far from shy; she can be a downright, demanding little rascal!

Father, I know you've told us to be bold in bringing our petitions to You in prayer. But I'm afraid there are times when my requests are not answered as soon as I think they should be and, like Fluffy, I'm insistent on an immediate answer. At those times, help me not to become demanding but develop patience knowing that You're never late in providing the answers at just the right time.

Different

For who maketh thee to differ from another?
I Corinthians 4:7 (KJV)

Fluffy has always been able to let herself out of a door. I don't know if that is an inborn instinct or not; but it's something I never taught her. However, I would like to teach her how to get back in again; but since I'm not a cat and can't see into the workings of her mind, I don't know how to proceed.

Our neighbors have two cats, on the other hand, who know how to get back inside but haven't been able to master the secret of letting themselves outdoors in the first place. If Fluffy would only come out of her antisocial shell and associate with Calico and Shoe, perhaps the three of them could teach one another their different skills and abilities!

Perhaps because I'm human, and humans have a tendency to want others to conform to their mold, I'm trying to force Fluffy to fit my specs rather than be herself.

The most miserable three months of my life was when I embarked on a new career and tried to become just like my boss who was held in high esteem by all who knew her. What a relief it was when I realized I couldn't be something

I wasn't—does that make sense?—and reverted to being my normal, ornery self once again!

I vaguely recall a couplet a relative, now deceased, wrote in my autograph album more than fifty years ago. It was something to the effect that,

Don't be what yo' ain't,
Jes' be what yo' is.
For if yo' am what yo' am not,
Then yo' am not what yo' is!

OK, Fluffy, because I like you the way you are, and because you're special to me, I guess I'll just let you be yourself, even though you haven't learned how to get back inside the house like Calico and Shoe.

Father, You created me in Your image—not someone else's, and because of that, I'm special to You. May I always remember that it's all right to be different just so long as I'm what You want me to be. I know that although You love me just the way I am, You also love me too much to allow me to remain that way, so are working on me daily to conform me to Your likeness. For that I thank You.

Dirty Paws

A man will always reap just the kind of crop he sows!
Galatians 5:7 (KJV)

When my landlord, Ben, utilized a sealant on our somewhat lengthy black-top driveway a couple years ago, we were unable to drive on it for two days. Naturally I told Fluffy not to walk on it, either. But then I figured she would automatically shy away from the ooey-gooey black, tar-like stuff. Not so! Not so! Instead, she delighted in deliberately walking on that sealer at every opportunity. I won't even try to describe what four white kitty paws look like after a few trips across wet blacktop! Of course, she reasoned that was the only way to get to her favorite haunts at the back of our spacious premises.

Now Fluffy could have reached the back yard via a detour through the front yard, then circling to the far side of the house and on to the garden. It wasn't that she didn't know the route, for she goes that way all the time whenever she wants to. But she wasn't changing her routine morning jaunt for anything, not even sealer on the blacktop!

I ask you, did you ever try to wash dried tar stuck on a cat's paws? Never, but never did I find anything that would dissolve the icky-looking stuff. I'm not expressing myself very eloquently, but I just can't think of a better word to describe the sealer than "stuff"—especially when it's on four white cat paws! Even Fluffy's vigorous ablutions didn't phase it. Her feet were a mess, in capital letters, but there was absolutely nothing we could do other than wait for it to gradually wear off.

I wonder when Ben's going to seal the drive again?

Father, how well I know that sin and bad habits, like Fluffy's dirty paws, leave indelible marks upon my life, marks that cannot be removed, as hers were, just by waiting. Thank You, Lord, for providing an instantaneous remedy through the Blood of Jesus Christ Who gave His life on the cross of Calvary that I might be saved and cleansed from all unrighteousness. And I know that when I've confessed my sin, no matter what it may have been, when You look at me through the precious Blood of Your Son, You see naught but a pure heart.

Don't Lose Sight

As for me, I look to the Lord.
Micah 7:7 (TLB)

Fluffy was in the hospital—just overnight, mind you. Nothing was seriously wrong with her; in fact, the doctor never did discover what caused her lengthy summer-time lethargy! I felt so sorry for her when I picked her up that I didn't have the heart to put her in her cat carrier which she detests passionately. So all the five miles home, she laid her little head in my lap while I carefully manipulated the controls of the car with one hand and lovingly stroked her with the other. Of course, I maneuvered my vehicle in and out among the back streets instead of taking the busy highway.

Once home, Fluffy jumped out of the car of her own accord, heeled and followed me upstairs like a dog adhering to obedience school lessons. *How had the vet trained her so fast in just one overnight session?* I asked myself. But that was just the beginning! From that moment on, she refused to let me out of her sight for the next couple of days.

As I reflect upon her constant diligence in following me, I am reminded of the Old Testament account of Elisha's refusing to leave Elijah at the last, steadfastly keeping his eyes upon his master until he saw his venerable predecessor taken to heaven in a chariot of fire.

Father, may I always look to You not only in times of trouble but also in times of peace and prosperity. Help me to keep my eyes securely and constantly fastened upon You in all situations and unhesitatingly follow wherever You lead.

Escapee

I can never be lost to your Spirit!
I can never get away from my God!
Psalm 139:7 (TLB)

Fluffy and I live in an upstairs apartment. Although we have a front entrance, we never use it as the car is parked at the back of the house. And why shovel a path through the deep western New York snows during wintertime? So, like me, Fluffy uses the back entrance—when she doesn't jump off the side porch, that is!

I try to keep the downstairs doors open for her in good weather even though it means daily trips for me up and down the unheated steep steps. Of course, I'll be the first to admit I need the exercise! Although the inside door at the foot of the stairs can be locked at any time, I usually just close it enough to latch part way. Then, when I return from shopping with my arms full of groceries, all I need do is shove it open with my foot or shoulder without setting the groceries down while I fumble for my keys.

Fluffy is no dummy. And every so often in cold weather when she finds that door partially latched, she'll work it open with her paw. For the life of me I can't figure out how a ten-pound cat can open a six-and-a-half-foot wooden door with one tiny paw—but she does! Nor can I comprehend how she can open a door from the inside but doesn't have the mental capacity to butt it open from the outside with that little hard head of hers whenever she wants to come back in! What a conundrum!

In cold weather, however, I close that outside door downstairs to conserve heat. So when Fluffy makes her occasional escapes, she's trapped in the lower entryway. If she'd only meow, my landlord and his wife would let her in their kitchen. But no, she just sits there until I miss her, even though it may be an hour or two. Those are the times I'm thankful she has a long, furry coat, so I know she won't get too cold, even in sub-zero weather.

And then she has the gall, believe it or not, to scold me when I eventually drag my arthritic limbs down the stairs to let her in! What an ungrateful "wretch!"

Father God, I'm so glad I can never be separated from You, for every moment You know where I am. You chart my path and guide my steps. Darkness cannot hide me from Your blessed face. How precious it is, Lord, to know that You have Your eyes upon me at all times and I can trust You to find me when I stumble and lose my way.

Falling in Love Again

See how very much our heavenly Father loves us.
I John 3:1 (TLB)

I love sales—garage sales, yard sales, household sales, moving sales, block sales, rummage sales—you name it. I guess you could say I love bargains! Especially when I can pick up coffee mugs for ten or fifteen cents each; and if it has anything to do with cats, I'll even splurge and pay a whopping quarter!

My favorite "kitty kups" are two special mugs prominently displayed in my glassed-encased china cabinet along with twenty-some collector's cat plates, all registered. Sculptured on the side of each of the mugs are two white kittens playing with pink balls of yarn against a backdrop of a blue afghan draped over the side of the cup. I didn't find those, of course, at any garage sale! Rest assured I will not be serving tea or any other beverage in those mugs—not even to my best friends!

On the other hand, I use the ten-and-fifteen-cent garage sale mugs on a regular basis. Hot chocolate tastes extremely yummy in the cup that has a frame on either side. One side depicts an overweight woman shaking her finger at her orange tabby, obviously berating her as she scolds, "Well, Fluffy, you've clawed the furniture for the last time! I'll not tolerate that behavior any longer!" That frame is labeled, "What we say to cats," and when I read it, I always give a sardonic snort and comment mentally, *Oh, yeah? I bet!* The second frame, on the other side of the cup, displays an identical picture of the nagging female and is labeled, "What cats hear." But the cat just sits there with a big grin on its face while the area that should contain her mistress' words is an absolute blank!

This morning I had my tea in a mug ringed with dancing cats sprouting little red hearts above their heads much like a halo. Around the rim of the cup are the words, "Every time I think of you, I fall in love all over again." Prejudiced cat owner that I am, as far as my relationship with Fluffy is concerned, truer words were never spoken!

Father in heaven, words cannot adequately convey my love to You for Who You are, for what You've done for me, and for all Your daily blessings. May I show by a life of willing obedience that truly I keep falling in love with You over and over again.

Feline Welcome

...(H)is father saw him coming.
Luke 15:20 (TLB)

I remember how passionately, as a child, I used to watch the clock until it was time for Father to come home from the lumberyard where he worked. Both noontime and 5:00 p.m. found me scanning the street eagerly for my first glimpse of him as he rounded the corner a half-block away. I'm sure I could have easily won the hundred-yard dash as I hurtled toward him with all the speed my small body could muster. It was difficult to decide who was more excited–Father or me, as we welcomed each other with open arms. I was too young, of course, to concern myself with the pleasure Father probably received from such an exuberant welcome. But all that changed when I became the proud "parent" of a cat: namely, Fluffy.

During warmer weather, Fluffy willingly follows me downstairs and watches me climb in the car, perfectly content to stay home while I run my daily errands. Whether my trips are short or long, I can be sure of one thing: she will be on hand to welcome me home. If she's on the side porch, she can see my car as I turn in the drive. If she's roaming around the back yard or asleep in the attic, she's apparently learned from the sound of the engine that it's my car turning in the drive, for she pays no attention to other vehicles that may pull in. If I'm gone for a few days and she's staying with my landlord, Ben will tell her shortly before it's time for my scheduled homecoming. She seems to understand, for she then demands to be outside where she waits expectantly for my return.

Fluffy may be just a cat, but what a thrill it is to know she's waiting for me, and to watch her amble toward my parked car knowing she'll be there to rub against my ankles in greeting just as soon as I unfasten my seat belt and open the door. Side by side we walk to the house, happy and rejoicing that we can be together once again.

Now, if only I could train her to carry in the groceries!

Father, it won't be long until You'll be calling Your children to their heavenly home. I can almost see You expectantly leaning over the portals of Heaven, arms longingly outstretched, waiting to welcome us one and all. What a glorious day that will be when I make that final run into the shelter and safety of Your loving embrace and hear You say, "Welcome home, Lois. Welcome home."

Finicky Appetite

...God sent them food to eat.
I Corinthians 10:3 (TLB)

Fluffy will eat turkey, but not chicken! Even so, the turkey has to be white meat, not dark. Guess we're kin to Jack Spratt and his "lovely" wife: Fluffy eats no dark meat, I eat no white; so between the two of us, we lick the platter clean—I mean we polish off a turkey with no problem! (I still refuse to let Fluffy help me lick dishes—I mean wash dishes.)

Fluffy will also eat kitty tuna but not "people" tuna although she'll lap the juice like she's dehydrated whenever I open a can of tuna for salad. She's even trained Willie, our landlady, to save tuna juice for her. In shopping for cat food, I must be sure any beef or ham I buy has gravy on it—that's OK; but I dare not get it without gravy!

I used to be able to entice her to do anything I wanted for a few pieces of kitty treat—Pounce, for example. But now that she's learned I'm blackmailing her with it, she has nothing to do with kitty treats. Oh, yes, she'll still eat them for Willie—but not for me! With me, her treats now consist of cheese, pop corn, pizza, even strawberries—if they're covered with Cool Whip, that is. Yes, I said, "strawberries!"

I ask myself repeatedly, *Who taught Fluffy to be so finicky?* Maybe I should change her name from "Fluffy" to "Fussy."

Thank You, Father, that I don't have to seek here and there for whatever kind of spiritual food I can find, some of which may be questionable, for You have provided all the spiritual nourishment I need in Your holy Word. May I always be content to eat at Your table, knowing that what You set before me, once I digest it, will provide spiritual strength and health which, in turn, will result in spiritual growth.

Cat Trivia

DISCRIMINATION (AS FLUFFY SEES IT)

When my human eats her food off the table but makes me eat mine off the floor—that's discrimination!

When my human refuses to let me eat out of the same dish she's eating out of at the same time—that's discrimination!

When my human enjoys giving me gifts but refuses my gifts of dead birds and mice—that's discrimination!

When my human uses a paper shredder all the time but won't let me shred the toilet paper—that's discrimination!

When my human knits and crochets but won't let me near the skeins of yarn—that's discrimination!

When my human plays with the dirty clothes from the laundry basket by throwing them in piles on the floor but won't let me romp in those piles—that's discrimination.

When my human won't let me climb the Christmas tree when every cat knows trees were made to climb—that's discrimination!

When my human warms food on the kitchen stove but won't let me keep warm by sleeping there—that's discrimination!

Flea Bitten Feline

The little foxes are ruining the vineyards.
Song of Solomon 2:15 (TLB)

Fluffy's never had a problem with fleas—until last year, that is. In fact, the vet claims that fleas are allergic to her! I always assumed it was the other way around! Try as hard as he could at her yearly checkups, he could find nary a sign of the illusive, pesky little monsters.

Last summer, however, the neighbors' cat found her way, uninvited, to my apartment, and made herself at home on my bed as often as she could. Naturally she couldn't come alone—had to bring her two little ones with her. I chased them home every time I found them. I scolded them; I tried to frighten them; I sprayed them with water, but nothing, absolutely nothing worked. And—you guessed it! They all had fleas! It wasn't long until Fluffy did, too!

A few years ago I worked for someone who owned and rented apartments; so I know some of the tricks for getting rid of fleas. Putting cucumber peels under the refrigerator, for example, sprinkling the rugs with borax, using flea sprays and shampoos, etc., etc. The borax took care of the carpeting, but not the cat. When I tried sprays on Fluffy, I got more bites and scratches than she got spray! At WalMart I picked up one of those little bottles where you snip off the end and just apply the liquid to the skin on the back of the cat's neck. That didn't work, either. Finally I turned to my trusty vet—for a price of course! But I did get rid of the fleas!

I guess it pays to be careful of the company you keep, whether you're a cat or a person!

Oops–have I been flea bitten by the internet bug? Ouch! How did that subject come up?

Little foxes, tiny fleas, daily activities, whatever—don't let yourself get bitten!

Father, help me seek Your face in all my activities and allow nothing, no matter how small it may seem, to come into my life that would rob me of Your blessing or lessen the time I spend with You.

Flower Pot Toys

Whereby are given unto us exceeding great and precious promises.
II Peter 1:4 (KJV)

"They're mine!" screams Fluffy to anyone who comes near the large ceramic flower pot I made when teaching ceramics many years ago. I painted a jungle scene all around the outside of the container and now use it as her toy box—toy canister would be more accurate, I guess. I'll never be able to unravel the workings of her mind, but somehow she knows that's HER flower pot and those toys are HERS and HERS alone.

If I'm too preoccupied to play with her for any length of time, in desperation she'll go to her flower pot and nuzzle through the soft playthings until she finds something that tickles her fancy. Sometimes she'll try to disentangle it from its surroundings by dipping a paw among the trinkets and carefully lifting out the desired toy. Other times she gives way to her inherent cannibalistic nature, grabs onto a coveted stuffed mouse and viciously throws it high in the air, trying to catch it as it falls. Or she'll try to shake the stuffing (literally) out of a crocheted Easter egg, then bat it back and forth from one room to another. I've found those eggs in the kitchen, under the bed, beneath the organ pedals, back in the closet, and a half dozen other places where she either can't retrieve them or tires of them! Stuffing, of course, is often neatly strewn in her wake, a fact which makes it easy to find the erstwhile egg, now nothing more than a glob of dirty, unraveled yarn.

As a rule, once the toys have been scattered throughout the house, Fluffy will have nothing more to do with them until I have gathered them all and put them neatly back into her ceramic flower pot. But, oh, the bending and the stooping that entails for my ever-aging body! How grateful I should be for the exercise!

I wonder if she counts all her toys to make sure I haven't missed any? After all, they do belong to her, you know! I think her favorite Gospel chorus must be a spinoff of "Every Promise In The Book Is Mine." Her rendition, however, is, "Every toy in the pot is mine; all the mice, all the eggs, they're all mine!"

Thank You, Lord, for the many precious promises You've given me in Your Word. Because every single one belongs to me, help me never to hesitate to claim them in my time of need. Truly they are all mine.

Fluffy Thoughts

How precious it is, Lord, to realize that you are thinking about me constantly! I can't even count how many times a day your thoughts turn towards me. And when I waken in the morning, you are still thinking of me!
Psalm 139:17, 18 (TLB)

How fortunate for both Fluffy and me that my pet-loving landlord and his wife live downstairs and are more than willing to take care of my precious cat whenever I go away for a few days. Although I know she'll get the best of care while I'm gone, my thoughts are about her more than I care to admit. Especially at night when there's no soft ball of fluff to sleep on the foot of my bed. My waking thoughts automatically turn toward her also; for when I'm home, she softly creeps up to my pillow in the mornings, lies down in front of my face and revs her "motor" full blast hoping, thereby, to get her breakfast. The shrill clang of the alarm clock isn't nearly so gentle a reminder of a new day. So when on vacation, my first waking thought is, *Has Willie* (my landlady) *fed Fluffy yet?*

Whenever I return to my motel room during the day, it's empty—no Fluffy waiting to rub against my legs and sing me her special welcome home song. The afternoon sun blazes in all its brilliance and I think, *Is Fluffy taking her daily sun bath on the edge of the desk or has she decided to keep Ben* (my landlord) *company on the front porch?* Dusk settles in quietly at the close of a long day and I question, *Is she alone in the apartment, now, and does she miss me?* And when I crawl into bed for the night and snuggle beneath warm blankets, I commiserate to myself, *How can I ever go to sleep with no Fluffy at the foot of my bed?*

I've never actually counted the number of times I've thought of Fluffy when I'm not with her, but I know, as numerous as they are, my thoughts don't begin to compare with the number of times the Lord thinks about me. The Psalmist David said he couldn't even add up the sum of God's thoughts toward him as they numbered more than the sand! Wow!

And as I think of Fluffy, my heart goes out in gratitude to a wonderful Lord and Savior who thinks about me continually. In fact, says Jeremiah 29:11 (KJV), *I know the thoughts that I think toward you, saith the Lord, thoughts of peace, and not of evil.*

O Lord, help me grasp the fact that You are thinking about me right now and that Your thoughts of me are more than can be numbered. Thank You because I have nothing to fear knowing Your desires and thoughts toward me are those of peace.

Fluffy, Fluffy, Quite Contrary

...(T)herefore thou art contrary.
Ezekiel 16:34 (KJV)

Truer words were never spoken about my precious Fluffy than those written above! In all honesty, though, I must admit that most of the time she is a submissive and obedient cat; but when she decides to assert her own will, look out!

Contrariwise, she's at her best (or should I say "worst") at night. Because I'm a "night owl"and seldom retire before midnight, Fluffy waits until I settle myself in my La-Z-Boy with a good book. Then she prowls to the front door and sticks her nose in the crack. She could give the door a nudge and it would open of its own accord; but no, she meows for me to come let her out. I try to ignore her, but those expressive eyes turn so pleadingly in my direction that I can no longer enjoy my reading. Begrudgingly I lay my book down, push the lap robe aside and walk over to let her out. As I open the screen door, however, she turns around haughtily and stomps off to the bedroom!

Once again I settle myself comfortably in my recliner, immersed in a fascinating story, and it's déjà vu. This time she wants out in the front attic. Again I disentangle myself from my afghan only to have her turn her back on the open door and haughtily stalk to sit in front of the kitchen door and give a plaintive, but triumphant "Me-e-e-ow !"

Ordinarily Fluffy wants to be with me except when she gets these spells of contrariness. At those times, if she's on the porch and I step out to rest in the swing, she prowls back into the house, even though it's cooler and more comfortable outside. On the other hand, if I follow her in, she returns to the porch! She couldn't have picked up that contrary streak from her owner, now, could she?

I think of that old couplet Mother taught me as a child:

As a rule, man's a fool;
When it's hot, he wants it cool.
When it's cool, he wants it hot,
Never pleased with what he's got!

Hmmmmm! I wonder—do I show that same characteristic in my Christian walk?

Father, there are times in my life when I try to do things my own way rather than seek Your face. Thank You for being so patient with me and for gently drawing me back into Your will. Help me to be submissive and obedient to You at all times, knowing that You always have my best interests at heart and make no mistakes.

Good Things Come in Small Packages

...(P)recept upon precept; line upon line.
Isaiah 28:10, 13 (KJV)

I've never had to worry about Fluffy jumping up on the kitchen table, even when she desperately wants a tidbit of whatever I'm eating. In fact, she seldom begs for food when I'm eating my meals at the table. Taking my food to the comfort of my easy chair, however, is a vastly different story!

The aroma of my succulent breakfast ham the other morning was one of the few exceptions when she drove me nuts with her begging. (Cats are known for driving their owners nuts!) She sat by my side on the floor and looked up at me with her big, soulful eyes that spoke more eloquently than words could ever have done. Not a single meow escaped her lips; but with every bite I took, her head swivelled back and forth in measured rhythm like an automated toy on a string. Plate to mouth; plate to mouth. Finally I could stand it no longer. Cutting off a good-size chunk of ham, I tossed it on the tiled floor by her side. *I would clean the small grease spot later,* I reasoned. But that grease spot grew like a weed nourished with Miracle Grow as she pushed the ham around and around, tossing it up in the air as though it were a mouse with which she was playing. Finally I figured out why she was acting so strange, seemingly wasting the perfectly good ham instead of eating it—she wanted me to cut it up into small, bite-size pieces! I had assumed that's what her teeth are for! After all, they are plenty sharp enough when she bites me if I dare play too roughly with her!

Sure enough, when I returned her ham cut into tiny morsels, she not only gobbled it up faster than I could eat my own, but also had the audacity to ask for more!

As I think about it, though, doesn't the kind Heavenly Father do the same for me spiritually?

Thank You, Lord, because You're just as careful with my spiritual food as I am with Fluffy's earthly food. You know just how much I can digest at one time; and instead of giving me big chunks of wisdom, understanding and knowledge all at the same time, knowing they might cause spiritual indigestion, you carefully and lovingly feed me precept upon precept, line upon line, here a little, there a little.

Grand Marshall

...(H)e is always thinking about you
and watching everything that concerns you.
I Peter 5:7 (TLB)

It happened one unforgettable Fourth of July when Fluffy was sick, and I phoned the vet. He told us to come in right away, that he was in the office only long enough to care for his overnight "guests" since it was a holiday. We rushed to the clinic, arrived in time to be treated, and then I tried my best to return home before our annual village parade began. But we didn't quite make it. The parade had just started when we reached the blinker light in the center of town. There I sat, the hot sun beating down on the car, and a sick cat sounding more like a dog baying at the moon than a tabby.

I looked longingly at our house nestled on the hilltop just a half block to my left, but fire engines, floats, pony-drawn carts, horses, tractors, and hay wagons moved slowly down the road nonstop while a guard prohibited all cross traffic. In desperation I sat on the horn until the patrolman directing traffic had no choice but to amble over to my car to see what the problem was. Rolling down the window just far enough to point out where we lived, I explained our unfortunate circumstances to him. And when he heard the shrieks from my sick, screeching passenger in the back seat, he actually stopped the parade and motioned us to continue homeward.

I don't know if I was successful in hiding my grin or not as I rounded the corner and turned up our drive. For Fluffy did what I never could have done—she stopped the parade as effectively as a Grand Marshall!

Thank You, Lord, for being such a loving, caring Father to Your earthly children. Thank You because You know all about our problems, large or small, and care enough about us that You'll go to any lengths necessary to meet our needs. What a wonderful God You are!

Happiness is...

Let me tell you how happy God has made me!
Isaiah 61:10 (TLB)

Someone once asked why a cat will stand and lift its paws up and down in one place on a person's body almost like marching in place. I've heard the procedure called both "kneading" and "pawing." Lately, however, I've adopted the term "jogging in place." At least that's what I do in the swimming pool—lift my paws, oops, I mean lift my feet up and down and "walk in place." It's good exercise for arthritic knees.

"Milk-treading," however, is a trait carried over from kittenhood days when kittens knead their mother's tummy to increase milk flow. Some cats will both knead and drool when petted. But forget the drooling as far as I'm concerned. The kneading, however, shows that the cat is happy and satisfied, likely recalling the best days of its life. How I enjoy seeing Fluffy demonstrate her contentment this way.

I once had a friend who refused to let her kittens show their delight in this manner. In my book, that constitutes cruelty to animals and should be reported to the SPCA if it would do any good! The fact that this particular acquaintance was my best friend at the time is beside the point. How I longed to "turn her in!" Fortunately, though, I heard a still, small Voice whispering, "Vengeance is mine, I will repay!"

What's wrong, I ask you, with Fluffy's being happy and showing it? Or any other cat, for that matter? Isn't that better than having her hiss and snarl at every one she encounters? Maybe my girlfriend (who moved to another part of the country years ago) is like some Christians who feel they shouldn't be happy and joyful, but think they are more spiritual if they wear a perpetual scowl and seldom smile!

Another acquaintance of mine lives next door to one of those long-faced, pseudo-Christians. I well recall the time that I, as a visitor, cracked a joke at a social gathering in the fellowship hall of the church just to "break the ice." But the ice didn't melt—it quickly grew into a 150-lb. block as Mrs. Sour-Puss jumped to her feet and reprimanded me by telling everyone present that her mother taught her there was a place for laughter but it wasn't in the church! I suppose my name for the dear, misguided woman—Mrs. Sour-Puss—isn't very Christlike, either. Forgive me, Lord.

In the meantime, Fluffy, go ahead and "do your thing" all you want, for when you're happy, I'm happy, too! Remember that old Ira Stanphill chorus? "Happiness is to know the Savior...

Happiness is the Lord!"

Father, I'm so glad You told us not once, but over and over again to rejoice in You and be glad. Thank You for creating me in Your image. The fact that I can smile, laugh, and be joyful tells me that those are Your characteristics, too. And when my heart is full of praise, I can't help but be happy in You.

Her Owner's Voice

...(T)hey know his voice.
John 10:4 (KJV)

My landlady took advantage of the gorgeous Spring day to sweep her front porch—I'm talking about ceiling, posts, cracks and crevices, the works! Noticing what appeared to be a swarm of small insects of some kind buzzing around my upstairs porch, I slipped downstairs to point them out to her. Our conversation ran the gamut of topics—what else would you expect when two women get together?

We're separated from the main highway by a row of evergreens, but because of the traffic we had to raise our voices to make ourselves heard. Suddenly, out of the corner of my eye, I caught sight of an orange and white streak hurtling across the yard in our direction. Fluffy, in spite of her age (We think she's somewhere around ten years old but don't know for sure!), had heard and recognized my voice. And now, faster than an Indy 500 racer, she came racing toward the comfortable, familiar sound. Was I pleased? You betcha! Pleased and proud as a banty rooster just learning to crow. What a smart cat I have! As I've said before, cats do take on the characteristics of their owners!

But am I really that smart? Do I recognize the Voice of my Savior as He speaks to me daily through the beauty of nature? Through the undeserved blessings that are mine? Through the howl of the tempest? The brilliance of lightning? The singing of birds? The gift of friends? The fellowship of a loving church family? Etc., etc., etc.

Father, I love You and thank You for promising that all things will work for my good. Help me to hear, recognize, and follow Your voice in every circumstance of life, whether good or bad, for I know that You are with me always and will not allow anything to come my way that You and I together can't handle.

Houseplants

So do not be attracted by strange, new ideas.
Hebrews 13:9 (TLB)

Fluffy enjoys her daily morning treks outdoors to feed on whatever kind of grass it is she uses to keep her digestive system operating properly. Personally, I prefer Tums even though I know "relief" is spelled R-O-L-A-I-D-S. In fact, my doctor insists I take two Tums daily to derive the benefit of the additional calcium. Oh, well, each to his own, I guess. Tums, Rolaids, or grass—whatever works for you.

Winter time is a different story, though; for here in western New York the snow is often two or more feet deep, hiding both the grass and Fluffy, should she ever attempt to navigate the glistening white powder that beckons and glitters so deceptively in the brilliant sunlight, but which would fail to hold her weight if she tried to walk on it. She still gets her greens, though—and I'm not talking about the popular herbal "greens," either. She eats my houseplants!

There are some house plants, I'm told, that are lethal for cats—dieffenbachia, for one, I believe. (I'm surprised I can spell it; and if one can't spell a word, how can you look it up in the dictionary to double check?) On occasion, I've gotten rid of some questionable flora just to be sure Fluffy won't be tempted with something poisonous. Inasmuch as possible, I have my plants in hanging containers during the colder months. But there is a limit as to how many flower pots one can have hanging from the ceilings and window frames! And it does no good to set a flower pot on a high piece of furniture; for if Fluffy wants it, she'll jump up and get it! It boils down to this: I can't put all green life out of her reach!

Her favorite indoor treats are spider plants. Mine thrive in the early morning sun and would make the window in the den so attractive if only I could let the "baby spiders" hang down in long clusters. But if you know anything about plants, you know how the ends of their leaves often turn an ugly brown if they're even so much as touched. All Fluffy has to do to taste them, is jump on the back of the day bed which sits beneath their spiraling foliage—and what a feast she has! As much as I hate to spoil the effect of the cascading "baby spiders," I've learned to wind them around the parent plant high above her head.

Undaunted, she works on my asparagus fern next, which hangs from a pole near the sewing machine. That's where she takes her daytime naps while I click away on my nearby computer. Although I keep the fern trimmed so it will branch out more fully, its fronds are still long enough so that all she has to do is lift her lazy, little head to find a tasty morsel!

I don't know whether Fluffy would actually eat a poisonous plant or not. But I do know that I'm not taking any chances. So I study houseplants carefully before adding new ones to my indoor greenhouse!

Father, there are so many new and strange doctrines in the world today. Help me not to accept every teaching set before me in the name of religion, but to try the spirits and ascertain that what I'm eating spiritually is in conformity with the truth of Your Word.

I Am His

...(T)hat they may be one, as we are.
John 17:11 (KJV)

Fluffy refuses to make friends with other cats. She hisses and spits whenever another furry feline makes its presence known. Should a tom approach her occasionally (even though she has been neutered), her cries resemble those of a banshee—not that I've actually heard a banshee wail! I've heard all I want to hear from Fluffy's wails!

I vividly recall the first time such an incident occurred! I was in my living room immersed in a religious romance—book, that is! The unearthly yowls that pierced the air swiftly brought me to my feet as my paperback went flying through the air. Racing onto the upstairs front porch, I peered over the railing, my breath coming in short spurts. Fluffy was lying on her side in the deep grass, making no effort to run but caterwauling loudly enough to cause a resurrection of the righteous dead in the cemetery behind our house! The noise rivaled that of fingernails scraping a blackboard! The tom fled, of course, when my high-pitched scream added to the ruckus—but Fluffy? Fluffy just lay there, prone, until I dashed downstairs—this was in my BA (before arthritis) days, cradled her in my arms, and carried her back upstairs to her safe haven, comforting her with "baby talk" all the way.

My next endeavor to instill in her the proper social graces for cats, was to introduce her to the neighbors' kittens who had just opened their eyes. Surely her mother instincts couldn't help but emerge when she saw such cute, tiny bits of fluff of her own kind, especially if they would try to cuddle up to her. But the minute she laid eyes on them, she began her hissing and spitting. Poor babies, they didn't know what to think. After all, THEIR mother had never talked like that to them!

It was my landlord who enlightened me as to the workings of Fluffy's mind. "She thinks you two are a team, Lois," Ben explained. "She figures you're all she needs and she's all you need. You're one. She doesn't know there's any difference between you and her." As one old Gospel song says, "I am His. He is Mine."

In light of Fluffy's loyal devotion to me, I ask myself, *Am I one with Christ as Fluffy thinks she's one with me?*

Father in heaven, may I always desire to be of one heart and mind with You and Your will for my life, even as You and Your Son are one. And because of this special oneness, may the world see Your love for them through my life in Christ.

Ignoring Me

...(W)ho could know the truth if they wanted to,
but they don't want to; they could hear me
if they would listen, but they won't.
Ezekiel 12:2 (TLB)

I was gone for only thirty hours, at a writers' conference nearby. Ben and Willie downstairs made sure that Fluffy was up in my apartment that first night—the only night, in fact—that I was gone. I had left plenty of food and water for her, and the next morning Willie went upstairs and let her out. I was home by 5:00 pm the second day.

As a rule, the minute I pull into our drive, Fluffy comes running to greet me, even when I've only been gone an hour or so on errands. But this time, she walked toward me slowly, then turned her head and deliberately went right on by without so much as a "how-do-you-do," a meow, or a grunt. She even refused to rub against my ankles. She saw me; she heard me—but she chose to ignore me! That was her way, you see, of punishing me for leaving her alone even though Ben and Willie take the best of care of her when I'm gone. I never have to worry when they're in charge.

Of course, her high-handed, disdainful attitude didn't

last long. I set my suitcase and tote bag on the ground and closed the trunk of the car. Her inquisitiveness got the best of her; and when she began snooping at my luggage, I simply picked her up, snuggled and kissed her. That's all it took, and she forgave me for abandoning her those few hours!

This was not the first time Fluffy had tried to punish me by ignoring my return. Possibly she thinks she needs to teach me that when I "run away," I am naughty and require discipline. And if I'm gone for several days, it takes a little longer before she'll have anything to do with me. On such occasions I go upstairs and wait patiently for her to return of her own volition. Once again, a little hugging and cuddling on my part helps her quickly recover from her little snit.

Father, how many times I act just like Fluffy. I have eyes to see, ears to hear, and could understand You if I really wanted to; but many times I ignore Your directions and try to do things my way, in my own strength. But I thank You, Lord, that when my limitations fail and I turn to You, You always pick me up, forgive me, and set my feet on the paths of righteousness once again.

I'll Always Have Time to Love You

I am convinced that nothing
can ever separate us from his love.
Romans 8:38 (TLB)

Fluffy has her daily devotions the same time I do! Our morning routine seldom varies. We make the bed, get dressed, put yesterday's dishes (still in the dish drainer) in the cupboard, get our breakfast—bacon and eggs for me (on the table, of course), seafood platter for her (in her special saucer on the floor), and then have our devotions.

My devotional guides and study Bibles have a permanent place on a stand to the right of my La-Z-Boy; pen, pencil and colored markers are within easy reach on the end table to my left. Fluffy watches me tilt my chair back, adjust the lap robe, and begin to write in my journal. That's her signal to jump up on my lap, step gingerly between the books spread all around, and force her way between my pen and my notebook.

A nuisance? Yes! But I never have the heart to push her off or even scold her. Instead, I lay my writing aside, remove the books, pick her up in my arms like a human baby, nuzzle my face in her warm, silky, white tummy, and murmur, "I'll always have time to love you, Fluffy." Satisfied with that wee bit of assurance, she "turns her motor on," curls up in a ball and snuggles among the soft, deep folds of the quilt, content to sleep until my devotions are finished.

How like my precious Jesus! He's never too busy to pay attention to me; and when I crawl up into His lap for assurance, I can hear Him say far more compassionately than I could ever speak to Fluffy, "Lois, I'll always have time to love You!"

Father, how I cherish Your voice whispering that You care for me. How comforting it is when Your arms of love encircle me, cuddle me, and assure me that nothing can ever separate me from Your wonderful, marvelous love.

Cat Trivia

LITTLE-KNOWN FACTS ABOUT CATS THAT EVERY CAT'S HUMAN SHOULD KNOW

Cats are the only animals that purr.

The average cat eats about 127,750 calories per year.

If humans slept as much as cats, they would work only from noon until 1:00 PM daily.

In America, more money ($3,000,000) is spent each year on cat food than on baby food.

No two cats have the same noseprints just as no two people have the same fingerprints.

Cats have left and right paws just as humans have left and right hands. Cats also tend to be left-pawed.

The average cat food meal equals about five mice.

CAT DISCIPLINE

In disciplining a cat, the discipline should be brief and sudden and such that will startle the cat. (Cats should NEVER be hit or spanked.)

Effective disciplinary measures could include slapping a ruler against a magazine, making a loud noise with a whistle or bicycle horn, or clapping your hands and hissing. You can also put a few pennies or small gravel in a tin can and shake it to produce a loud noise. And don't forget to try a squirt gun.

Double-sided carpet tape can be placed temporarily on woodwork or furniture to break a cat of sharpening its claws at that location.

I'm Not My Own

Ye are bought with a price.
I Corinthians 7:23 (KJV)

All good cat owners will readily admit they don't own their cats—their cats own them and quickly train them to become "cat slaves!"

Ever since I was obliged to put my last cat to sleep because of a terminal illness, I decided I would never get another, for I didn't want to go through the trauma of parting with a furry companion again. So when friends wanted to give Fluffy to me, I took her, not because I really wanted her, but because I felt sorry for the "poor thing." She had had several homes—I never did learn how many—and my heart went out to the rejected little orphan. It wasn't that she was unattractive or mean. To the contrary, she was a beauty to behold and had a most gentle nature. Nor had she been mistreated by prior owners. It just happened that someone in each family was allergic to long-haired cats—and Fluffy has long hair!

I kept her for a few weeks, but somehow it didn't seem as though she really belonged to me. She just wasn't my cat. After all, I hadn't picked her out, nor had I named her. I felt as though I was just another "dumping ground" for her!

Then I learned that her original name was Scruffy. My friends who brought her from Canada had changed her name to Fluffy as they felt she was too pretty just to be a Scruffy! So I thought maybe if I renamed her again, she would seem more like my own. But even that didn't make her mine.

Somewhat reluctantly, I returned her to my friends and then learned they were going to place an ad in the local newspaper and give her away to complete strangers. That I couldn't handle, so once again I brought her home, this time to stay whether she belonged to me or not!

Later that summer, Fluffy contracted some type of illness after playing among the weeds in a vacant lot. I don't recall the details now, but I remember that I spent between $200 and $300 on medicine, shots, and veterinarian's bills for her! And guess what? After that, there was no question about it—she belonged to me! At last she became my very own cat—I mean, she became my owner, for she had been bought with a price!

That was when Fluffy began singing her kitty version of a once-popular chorus:

Now, I belong to Lois;
Lois belongs to me.

(She always gets the words of gospel songs mixed up!)

Thank You, Lord Jesus, because I am not my own. I've been bought with a price—the price of Your very life's blood. Thank You that I belong to You, and You belong to me–"not for the years of time alone, but for eternity."

Increased Understanding

...(B)e filled with. . .spiritual understanding.
Colossians 1:9 (TLB)

Evidence from lab experiments indicates that cats possess a high level of intelligence. I believe this to be true, for Fluffy has often proved that even in deep sleep, her brain is as active as when she's awake.

R & R (rest and relaxation) is an important part of a cat's life, and one evening she had just snuggled down into the soft nest she had made on an old comforter thrown across my lap. I looked forward to a relaxing half hour of reading before turning in for the night, for I, too, enjoy R & R. I had only skimmed a few pages of my book when I noticed that she was already asleep—so I thought! Continuing to read, I stealthily reached over to the stand by my side and picked up my cup of steaming hot apple-cinnamon tea, not noticing the red pen that rolled around once its barricade had been removed. In a flash Fluffy was wide awake and snaked her little paw out to play a game of bat and chase with that pen! It was still on the comforter, and

I wanted it to stay within reach.

I ask you, did you ever try to holler, yell, scream, or even cry out "No, No!" at the same time you took a sip of hot tea? I couldn't even swat at her as I was holding my book with one hand and a full cup of hot beverage with the other! Because I had to act fast, without thinking I uttered a guttural "Hunh-uh" never once opening my mouth and choked down the tea all at the same time! To my astonishment, Fluffy ducked her head, withdrew her paw from temptation, and demurely settled back on my lap, her halo firmly in place once again!

Another phrase—"Hunh-uh"—added to her vocabulary, I exulted. She learns fast and understands more than I give her credit for, I guess!

Father God, in the name of Jesus I ask that You would make me wise about spiritual things and help me understand what You want me to do that I might always please and honor You by the way I live while all the time I learn to know You better and better.

Instant Replay

...(H)is lovingkindness begins afresh each day.
Lamentations 3:23 (TLB)

Although Fluffy usually drifts into slumberland curled up against my feet, it is not unusual for me to find her sound asleep on the pillow next to me when I awaken. Because I'm not a heavy sleeper, that can be several times a night. At those times she's so sound asleep that she apparently isn't aware of my slipping out of bed, making my way to the kitty litter—mine, that is, not hers—and silently creeping under the covers again. It gives me a great sense of accomplishment to perform this nightly ritual, for it's the only time I can "pull a fast one" without her knowledge!

More likely than not, however, when I come pattering back to bed, she's so cute that I just have to pet her. I know it disturbs her sleep, but she can go back to shut-eye land easier than I. And if she wants to sleep late in the morning to make up for her lack of sleep (which she never does), well, that's her prerogative, too!

But there's one thing I can always count on at these nightly rendezvous. No matter how soundly she has been sleeping, the moment—and I mean the exact moment I touch her, she shifts her "motor" into high gear! During the day, however, it may take her a few seconds to get her "engine" revved up. But not in the middle of the night—unless she's ill, of course!

Somehow I've latched onto the phrase "instant replay" to describe her nighttime singing. And although she may or may not be too far lost in dreamland to hear and understand me, before snuggling back under the blankets to finish my own interrupted slumber, I fondly nuzzle her neck and whisper, "There's that 'instant replay' again."

Thank You, Father, for Your mercies that are new each day. Thank You because each morning is an "instant replay" of Your bountiful blessings and tender care of Your people. May I never take Your benefits for granted but recall each favor as a repeat performance of Your marvelous love for me.

Intelligent But Not Too Bright

...(W)hen I want to do what is right,
I inevitably do what is wrong."
Romans 7:21 (TLB)

A cat's IQ, they say, is surpassed in the animal kingdom only by monkeys and chimps. It's times like tonight, however, that make me question that statement!

As night wrapped its dusky stillness around a gorgeous, sun-bathed day, Fluffy left her self-appointed task of sitting at my feet helping me write these devotions and slipped out to the front porch to watch the nocturnal creatures emerge from their daylight hiding places.

During the day I leave the porch door open so she can come and go at her pleasure. But when evening shadows deepen, I pull the screen door almost shut so the mystic insects of the dark will not feel they have an open invitation to enjoy the warmth and light of my indoor reading lamp.

I've bragged about Fluffy's intelligence (derived from close association with my side of the family, of course) which is evident when she pushes her head against the screen door and lets herself out on the front porch at night.

And when she's ready to come back inside, she sticks her little white paw between the door jamb and the screen door and pulls it to her just enough to widen a crack sufficient for her to squeeze through and come back inside. I don't know where she learned this trick; it must be that innate cleverness she possesses. (Possibly another trait she's picked up from her owner?)

Someone once said that cats are dogs with a college education. While I can't vouch for that, I've read that if cats would only use their God-given intelligence, they would be far more valuable to the U.S. Government than dogs are! (That "gr-r-r-r" I hear is coming from the dog lovers who've ventured to open this book.)

Similarly there have been many times when Fluffy has trotted downstairs and let herself outside. She reverses the process at this door, which opens inward and uses her paw to pull the door toward her. But somehow she can't learn to butt against it with her head when she wishes to come back in! And my arthritis discourages me from getting down on the cement porch floor and teaching her how it's done! If she can open the upstairs porch door and come back inside, why, I ask you, can't she do the same thing downstairs? This seems to shoot holes in my theory of intelligence imbibed from her owner. Well, anyway, she may be intelligent but just isn't too bright at times!

My face burns with shame as I confess that occasionally I'm just like Fluffy in my walk with the Lord. I'm smart enough to know what's right, but not always bright enough to do what I know I should!

Father in Heaven, thank You because Jesus Christ has set me free from slavery to my deadly lower nature. When I am tempted to do things in my own strength, may Your precious Holy Spirit remind me to walk in the paths of righteousness for Your Name's sake.

It Works Every Time!

And when you draw close to God,
God will draw close to you.
James 4:7 (TLB)

For Fluffy and me, it works both ways. Whichever makes the first move to get attention, the other responds in like manner. Her favorite way to get me to pet her is to curl up on the floor in a half-moon and stretch all four paws toward me. She's just too cute to resist, and she knows that will generally stop me in my tracks for a petting session regardless of how busy I may be.

On the other hand, I've found a foolproof way to get her to jump on my lap—not that she usually needs encouragement to do so. If she won't come at my insistent, "Uppy, uppy, Fluffy," I threaten her. "Guess I'll have to blackmail you, then," I say resignedly. She either hasn't learned what that means or ignores me as she waits for the next step in the oft-repeated scenario.

Now the tables are turned as I pretend to ignore her and stick my nose back in whatever book I'm reading. At the same time, I slowly snake my hand to the edge of the armrest on my La-Z-Boy and nonchalantly hold forth her wire kitty brush, all without saying a word.

It never fails! In a moment or two she gives her special little grunt, stretches luxuriously, and slowly creeps to my chair. I still refuse to meet her glance, for that seems to break the spell and she walks away. But if I ignore her long enough, she bounds onto my lap and begins to sing before I even touch her with the brush! And with a good brushing, which she dearly enjoys, she's content to curl up and go to sleep while I use her for a book rest.

It works every time!

Thank You, Father, because You never fail; Your Word works every time. You're the same yesterday, today, and forever. And at those seasons when I sense a deep desire to know Your presence in my life, all I have to do is draw nigh to You; for it never fails—that's when You draw nigh to me. Thank You, Lord, Thank You.

Just Ask

Ask, and it shall be given you.
Matthew 7:11 (KJV)

Fluffy doesn't meow for things too often. She generally gets what she wants just by sitting and looking at whatever it is she desires. Does she need to go outdoors? She sits and looks at the kitchen door. Does she want to go out on the porch for a sun bath? She sits and stares at the front door. Does she want to go prowling around in the attic? She sits at the attic door and fastens her gaze on it intently. After all, every cat knows that a door will eventually open if you stare at it long enough! As doorman, I'm her solution to the door problem—she just doesn't leave me any tips! Never once does she stop to consider how spoiled she is, although I, as her owner often lament, "How did that cat get so spoiled anyway?"

I wish I could get things that easily! How wonderful if just "looking at" a car would produce a brand new, bright red Dodge Caravan sitting in my drive. Or staring at my credit card statement would pay it off in full. Or following the flight of an airplane as it wings a path through the sunny skies would drop a round-trip ticket to U.S.A. Anywhere in my mail box. Apparently I don't have Fluffy's charm of birthing something into existence just by visualizing it!

What Fluffy doesn't realize, however, is that meowing to get back inside would be the equivalent of saying, "Open, Sesame." No, she just patiently sits outside the closed door and waits—who knows how long—for me to take pity on her and open the door, hoping she's there. Sometimes she's ready to return; other times she's nowhere in sight. But oh! the extra steps that causes me!

I did tell you she's one smart cat, didn't I? Harvard material? Takes after her owner? I'd never admit, though, that her "mother" is not a quick learner, either, at times—especially when it comes to spiritual things.

Invariably I tell Fluffy when she finally does appear, "All you have to do is meow, you know." And God continually reminds me, "Lois, all you have to do is ask, you know."

Forgive me, Father, for not always asking You for the help I need, especially since You've told me over and over in Your Word to do so. Help me to remember that because I'm a child of Yours, it's not only my privilege but also one of my God-given rights to come boldly before the throne of grace that I might find help in my times of need.

Kat Konsideration

And let us consider one another.
Hebrews 10:14 (KJV)

Consideration is an attribute that parents need to instill in the lives of their children. I'm not sure how that works in cat families. Perhaps pet owners should try to develop the quality of "eti-cat" in their feline companions. In any event, Fluffy has been most considerate of children so long as they don't tease her.

I've seen her let children just learning to walk pick her up and try to hold her even though she was almost as big as they were. They could only grasp her underneath her front legs, and her body and tail would almost drag the ground as they tried to toddle around the yard with their fluffy burden. Not once would Fluffy struggle to free herself from their grip, although it would have been an easy feat for her to simply jump out of their grasp, knocking them over as she did so. When the babies would eventually release their hold on her, instead of darting away from their eager grasp, she would curl up on the ground in a half-moon shape, begging for more attention, while her facial expression clearly said, "Let's do it again!" Naturally I keep my eagle eye on such situations to ascertain that she is not being harmed in any way.

If both adults and children are around, guess to whom she gravitates? The little ones! When the neighbor children come over, she leaves me and goes to them. The only caution I have for youngsters—adults, too, for that matter—is not to tickle Fluffy on her soft, white tummy—I'm the only one who can get by with that.

I have but one question. Who taught Fluffy to be considerate of and gentle with tiny tots? If you ever find out, I sure wish you'd let me know!

Dear Lord, help me always to be considerate of others, both children and adults, rich and poor, in all situations, thereby letting them see the compassion and love of Christ flowing from my life to theirs.

Kat Conversation

I will talk to you there.
Ezekiel 3:22 (TLB)

I've read that cats have the capacity to understand upwards of fifty different words and phrases. Seems to me Fluffy understands a lot more than that! Why, my landlord will tell her what time I'm expected to come home after I've been gone a day or so, and when the time comes, she jumps off her chair, goes to the door and meows to go outdoors and wait for me!

At night she jumps on the foot of my bed. More likely than not, she leaps onto the night stand, next to the window, to survey her backyard territory from her second-story advantage. When she is satisfied that all is well, she creeps back to her favorite spot at my feet. Then the conversation begins.

"Come talk to me, Fluffy," I sometimes coax, knowing full well what her response will be. Other times I invite, "Want to come cuddle a while?"

A small grunt signals velvety footsteps finding their way over the rough terrain of the covers toward the head of the bed. I lift the blankets to simulate a tent, and she crawls underneath, curving her lithe body into an arc that just fits into the curve of my arm. Sometimes even during the middle of the night, I am awakened by her wet little nose trying to burrow into the protecting haven of my arms beneath the sheet.

She never stays long—just a few minutes. No doubt her long hair makes the confines too hot for an extended visit. She soon wiggles out from under the bedclothes, pauses just long enough for a goodnight kiss, then proceeds to find my feet and cuddle against them for her night's sleep.

It's possible to converse with any cat, you know. What do Fluffy and I talk about during our nightly conversations? I'll never tell. That's a secret known only to Fluffy and me. But we get a lot of things settled. As an old hymn says, "A little talk with Jesus makes it right, all right."

How thrilled I am, Lord, to know that You, the God of the universe, are willing to talk with me any time, anywhere, about anything. Oft times our conversations are too personal for the ears of outsiders; but there's nothing, absolutely nothing that I cannot share with You. Thank You, Father, for the great privilege of communing with You one on one.

Katnip Kapers

O how love I Your law!
Psalm 119:97 (Amp.)

Fluffy's favorite toy is a catnip box I bought for her many years ago. I'm surprised she hasn't ruined it by now the way she plays with it. Eighteen inches long, four inches wide, and two inches high, the box boasts hundreds of tiny holes and appears to be filled with rows of corrugated cardboard. (At least that's what I used when I made a similar one for Fluffy's neighbor cat.) You can imagine the heady aroma that teases her sensitive nostrils when all those holes are filled with catnip which I replace on a regular basis.

After she sniffs the catnip, she really gets "drunk"; but like the drunk who learns to hold his liquor, Fluffy has learned to hold her catnip. Her contortions and antics are as good as those of the acrobats in the Ringling Brothers circus! Thank the good Lord for a Hammond organ; for I discovered that to keep Fluffy from pushing, shoving and pulling that box all over the apartment, as well as spilling its contents over the carpet, I could wedge it against the organ pedals, the organ bench, and the underneath side of the organ! Even without moving her beloved treasure, she still manages to sprinkle the catnip liberally around the living room as she first rolls on top of the box, then on the floor.

Not being overly fond of housekeeping, I shake my head in hopeless despair every time she plays her catnip games. When she staggers off in sheer exhaustion after falling into a drunken stupor, I reluctantly drag out my trusty vacuum cleaner and clean up the catnip she so liberally sprinkled across the room. That's when she does the disappearing act under the bed, for she hates the whirring of the sweeper.

Now, why, I ask you, can't she associate that dreaded noise with her catnip clownishness and stop making all that unnecessary katnip klutter! Is there such a thing as "human catnip," I wonder, that produces a wacky, daydreamy state of ecstasy?

Father, when I see how much Fluffy enjoys catnip, I have to search my heart and ask myself if I love You proportionately? Create within the depths of my being a hunger and thirst for You and Your will that will not let me be satisfied with anything less than all that You have promised me in Your blessed Word.

Kopy Kat

The pupil should be satisfied to become like his teacher.
Matthew 10:25 (Williams)

The first time I ate a dish of ice cream after Fluffy came to live with me was a hot, humid summer afternoon, and I was relaxing in my La-Z-Boy in front of the fan. When I finished my cool treat, I followed my long-standing custom of setting the empty dish on the floor, fully intending to carry it to the kitchen and wash it when I got up.

But I had forgotten I was no longer living alone, and Fluffy, bless her heart, decided to show me what a good dish washer she was! It took me a few moments to figure out what was going on when I heard the gentle sound of her little pink tongue pushing the spoon around. By the time I realized that she, too, was enjoying a midday snack of ice cream, she had the dish pretty well cleaned.

Since I'm the only person in my household, I wait until after my evening meal to wash all my dishes for the day. Grimacing in disgust, I set the empty ice cream saucer on the kitchen counter and reminded myself to be more watchful in the future and not put empty food dishes on the floor. I went about my afternoon duties and soon forgot the incident.

The stifling heat quashed any desire to cook a meal that evening, and I put aside all thoughts of either a balanced diet or my tendency towards high blood sugar and opted for another serving of butterscotch ripple ice cream. *Why dirty another clean saucer?* I reasoned to myself as I retrieved the ice cream from the freezer. *It's too hot to wash any more dishes than necessary!*

A fleeting glance at the clock revealed it was also time for the evening news. Quickly I reached to the counter top, grabbed the saucer I had used at noon, filled it with ice cream, and nibbled away while catching up with the news. It was during a commercial that I realized I was eating from the same dish that my new four-legged companion had so kindly washed for me earlier in the day! With a shriek that not only could have been heard a block away but also sent Fluffy running for cover, I jumped to my feet and went running to the garbage pail with the rest of my supper!

When Fluffy dared to creep out of hiding, she looked at me as much as to say, "What's wrong? You ate from that dish, and I'm just following your example."

Thank You, Father, for giving me Jesus, the one, true example to follow in my daily spiritual walk. May I, in turn, be an example of Your loving kindness to my fellow men and all those who follow in my footsteps.

Life of Ease

Woe to them that are at ease in Zion.
Amos 6:1 (KJV)

I'm honored to be living in one of the historic houses of New York State's Chautauqua County. Not only is there a plaque on one of the downstairs porches proclaiming this fact, but a picture of our stately home also graces the frontispage of the book *Nineteenth Century Houses in Western New York.*

Built in 1847, the house boasts two round windows—one in my front hallway and the other in my bedroom. Visitors are always intrigued by the way those windows disappear right into the wall when I raise them! Fluffy, on the other hand, takes advantage of the open bedroom window in warm weather by lying on the window sill to catch the cool summer breezes that our hilltop seems to attract no matter how stifling the heat may be. She reminds me of that old nursery rhyme about Wynken, Blynken and Nod with its accompanying illustrations that showed one of the children asleep in a half moon, for the bottom of that round window sill is just that shape—half moon!

One Memorial Day weekend the weather was perfect for picnics, parades, and what have you, so I was delighted that it was warm enough for Fluffy to roam outdoors from morning to evening. But she had a different idea! As I made the bed, smoothed out the spread and plumped up the contrasting decorator pillows, she came back inside and succeeded in hampering my progress as she walked across the bed and then jumped over into that round window! Flattening herself to accommodate its half-moon contours, she settled down for the day, perfectly content to survey the backyard from the heights of our second story apartment. Ignoring Ben, our landlord, who called to her from his lawn chair as he sat in a patch of warm, bright sunshine directly beneath the window, she stretched luxuriously and settled down for a comfy nap.

After all, why should she expend the energy to walk downstairs and patrol the premises when she could just as well perform her duty from the ease and leisure of that round window!

Heavenly Father, may I never be guilty of relaxing my guard and taking my ease concerning spiritual matters. There's a work to be done, and the only hands and feet You have to do that work are those belonging to Your children. Help me not to shirk my God-given responsibilities but be faithful in the labors to which You have called me.

Little By Little

...(H)ere a little, and there a little.
Isaiah 28:10, 13 (KJV)

Fluffy has had more than her share of sickness as far as I'm concerned. Her illnesses take a far greater toll on me than they do on her!

Once when she was recovering from a lengthy bout of indigestion, which even the vet admitted she was unable to diagnose properly, I purchased a particular species of lily plant that had been advertised in the newspaper. Its flowers were supposed to be gorgeous, and I could hardly wait to see the magnificent blossoms. I planted it carefully and followed closely the detailed instructions for its care.

Then one day Fluffy took a nibble from one of the leaves of my new purchase, but I didn't think too much about it. After all, she hadn't been going downstairs for a few weeks to get the grass which usually calmed her stomach, so I figured there was no harm done to my healthy plant when she occasionally nibbled on the end of a leaf. It was just good to see her take an interest in her surroundings again.

Within a couple days, though, Fluffy had a relapse. I wracked my brain trying to figure out why. Then it dawned on me—that new plant I had so proudly placed on the front porch a few days before was the culprit! It was a member of the Dieffenbachia family—a plant genus that could be fatal to cats! Little by little it was doing its deadly work in Fluffy's tummy!

That plant quickly found a new home with a friend who had no pets. No, I never did get to see those blossoms, and know what? It really didn't matter! For I didn't want anything around that would harm my baby, no matter how exotic it might be!

Father, there are so many seemingly unimportant things that can sap my spiritual life, little by little—a wrong attitude here, a hasty word there, neglect of Bible reading and prayer, a good deed left undone—on and on and on. Help me to guard these areas of my life carefully and be sensitive to Your Voice as You continually remind me to be diligent in working out my own salvation.

Look Alikes

Let us make man. . . after our image.
Genesis 1:26 (TLB)

In her younger days, one of Fluffy's favorite resting places was on top of the six-foot bookcase just outside my office door. She made the climb easily in three steps—first from the floor to the chair, next from the chair to the filing cabinet. Then, carefully measuring the final jump, she would wiggle her little fanny, work up momentum, and make the final leap across the intervening space and onto the bookcase. On one occasion, in fact, I was able to photograph her in mid air as she made her daring jump across the perilous chasm from bookcase to floor. Never once did she lose her footing. She would curl up and sleep on that bookcase for hours, especially in cold weather when the heat of the furnace would blow directly across the room on her, ruffling her fur while acting like a soft, downy blanket.

For years, even before I had Fluffy, I have hung a large cat calendar on the side of that particular bookcase, and each month enjoyed having another adorable cat picture gracing the decor.

One winter evening as I walked through the house and cast a casual glance at her, ensconced in her usual place high above her surroundings, I was astonished to see not one, but two cats. Both were orange and white with long hair, had their heads resting on their paws, and were staring intently at me with their large, expressive eyes, one directly beneath the other!

Because I had been deeply engrossed in my work, my mind refused to change channels quickly enough to comprehend what I was really seeing. My thoughts raced in all directions. *Had a second Fluffy somehow found her way into the apartment? Why did my Fluffy allow her to stay since she hated other cats?* And *how could the second Fluffy be looking at me from the top shelf of the bookcase since it was full of books?*

Rooted to the spot, I shook my head in bewilderment until I finally realized that the "second Fluffy" was the picture on the cat calendar!. When I had turned the calendar page a few days prior, I had failed to notice that the new picture was a replica of a younger version of my very own Fluffy!

At the close of the year, I framed that particular picture which now hangs on my office wall. And at this writing, Fluffy is sleeping on the sewing machine while her calendar likeness lovingly watches over her.

Father, I stand in awe when I contemplate the fact that I was created in Your image, in Your likeness. Grant that others may always be aware of that likeness, not because of physical attributes but because my attitudes and actions are directed and controlled by You thereby displaying the likeness of Christ in my life.

Meticulous Eater

(B)e ye stedfast, unmoveable.
I Corinthians 15:58 (KJV)

I've never been able to resist a bargain. Guess that's why I like rummage sales—especially bag sales! You know, those last minute sales where you pay only $1.00 for all the junk you can stuff in a brown grocery bag? And have I ever learned to stuff the junk! I sometimes think I'm a professional stuffer! (Perhaps "junk dealer" would be more appropriate!) I've learned all the secrets of the trade such as rolling clothes and slipping them down into the empty crevices of a bag until there is not one iota of space wasted! Then, too, no one seems to care if you have your bag overflowing with junk, even if it's hanging down over the sides! Obviously, no one uses the word "junk" in an advertisement, but I don't know any other words besides "stuff" and "junk" that adequately describe the contents of one of those bags once I have it filled!

It was at just such a bag sale that I picked up a nice divided pet dish–a plastic dish that holds food on one side and water on the other. Of course, I set the dish on top of my already heaped-up and overflowing bag. But at home when

I transferred Fluffy's food to this marvelous dish, I discovered she would drop pellets of dry food that were in one side of the dish into the water on the other side—whether accidentally or intentionally, I'm not sure! What a sloppy mess that was for me to contend with! Nor did the water and food run out at the same time. This made cleaning the dish a nuisance. Eventually I compromised by putting dry food in both compartments of the dish and using a separate container for water.

Now, I ask you, who taught Fluffy to be meticulous in her eating habits? For without fail, since she's gotten this new bowl, she'll eat from the right side of the dish first. Only when that is empty will she start eating from the left compartment. *Well, at least,* I console myself, *she's consistent!* (She's a persistent little rascal, also, I might add!)

Oh that I could learn to practice that same consistency and persistency, too, in my Christian life!

Father, help me to be steadfast and unmoveable in my walk with You, always abounding in the work of the Lord, knowing that such qualities will produce the strength of character in my life that You desire.

Dear Tabby's Syndi-cat-ed Column

Catsville, U.S.A.
By Ruth K. Allison

Dear **Tabby:** I was going to write to Dear Abby with my problem, but she wouldn't know as much as you. My human mother mixes two kinds of dry food for me, but I don't like the one kind. What shall I do? **Wondering**

Dear **Wondering:** Be selective as you eat. Just take the tidbits you like. When the undesirable pieces accumulate enough, your human mother will catch on! **Tabby**

* * * * *

Dear **Tabby:** I don't have anyone to play with, and it gets pretty lonesome around my house. Should I run away? **Lonely**

Dear **Lonely:** Don't run away. It is very likely that your family makes up their beds every morning. Wait until they do, and surprise them by jumping between the sheets. But you will have to be fast. When they dive for you, try to get wound up in the sheets. This can become a very exciting game. You may be able to prolong the fun for several minutes. **Tabby**

* * * * *

Dear **Tabby:** I like to watch my human mother wash her hair in the bathroom, but I also want to listen to my daddy play his violin at the same time. How can I be in two places at once? **Confused**

Dear **Confused:** Lie in the bathroom door with part of your body inside and part out, and you can observe both activities. For further information on this subject, you need to get a copy of my new book, **"The Best of Two Worlds." Tabby**

* * * * *

Dear **Tabby:** I am an INDOOR cat and do not get enough exercise in our small house. How can I keep my body young and nimble? **Stiff**

Dear **Stiff:** If there are small throw rugs on the kitchen floor, run and land on them very fast. Often they will scoot across the floor and make perfect skateboards. But then run for your life, especially if anyone is working in the kitchen. **Tabby**

* * * * *

Dear **Tabby:** My drinking water is changed every other day, but I crave fresh water after every meal. Is there any solution? **Thirsty**

Dear **Thirsty:** Check the bathrooms. If you hear dripping water, curl up in the lavatory and suck the faucet. It is delightful. You will think you are a nursing kitten again. **Tabby**

* * * * *

Dear **Tabby:** How can I spice up my life while my people are away at work all day long? **Bored**

Dear **Bored:** In nice weather, see whether you can slip out unnoticed once in awhile when they leave in the morning. If this is not possible, unwind the rolls of toilet paper in all the bathrooms. Just grab the loose end and start running. It's lots of fun! **Tabby**

* * * * *

Dear **Tabby**: My family sleeps late. How can I get them up at a decent hour? **Impatient**

Dear **Impatient**: Find their bare feet under the covers and play with their toes. This almost always works. **Tabby**

* * * * *

Dear **Tabby**: How can I get my owner to quit using white yarn and start using dark purple when she knits? I can hardly see the white but nearly "go wild" with delight playing with the dark colors. **Poor Eyes**

Dear **Poor Eyes:** Humans who knit usually have several colors of yarn stashed away. Look for the storage place, select the skein you like, and drop it at the feet of your owner. Be purr-sistent, and if she has a high enough IQ, you will soon communicate. **Tabby**

* * * * *

Dear **Tabby:** When I need my sleep, my mother likes to sit near me on the end of the sofa by the lamp and knit. How can I snooze in peace while she is constantly pulling yarn out of a skein. It is very tantalizing. **Sleepy**

Dear **Sleepy:** Try to beat your mother to her favorite spot on the end of the sofa by the lamp. If she wants you to move, cry a little and pull the "sick act." This may persuade her to feel sorry for you and go somewhere else with her knitting. **Tabby**

* * * * *

Dear **Tabby:** When I am on my daddy's lap, I don't like it that he uses me for a desk to hold the newspaper while he does the crossword puzzle. This happens almost every morning. Any suggestions? **Purr-plexed**

Dear **Purr-plexed:** Start squirming. He'll stop! **Tabby**

* * * * *

Dear **Tabby:** Is there any way to let my owners know I want them to share their fluffy white kernels with me at bedtime when they have their snack? **Neglected**

Dear **Neglected:** Those kernels are called popcorn. Get

as close to it as you can and sniff. Try a Meow or two. It often helps to scoop a pawful out of the bowl if you can be fast enough. **Tabby**

* * * * *

Dear **Tabby:** How can I get my family to put a chair or desk by the window so I can see out? **Confined**

Dear **Confined:** Try climbing the curtains. When they get shredded enough, it will encourage your family to arrange the furniture more conveniently. **Tabby**

* * * * *

Dear **Tabby:** My mother tries to get me to play with my tail by wiggling it in front of my nose. That's for kittens. I'm a grown cat! Am I "nuts" or is she? How can I get her to stop? **Mature**

Dear **Mature:** Every time she does this, cross your paws in front of your eyes and refuse to look. She will soon notice that you are not interested. **Tabby**

CALLING ALL CATS

Do you have a frustration or perplexing situation? For good advice (Well, sometimes it's good), address your problem to **DEAR TABBY.**

Mind Reader

The Lord knoweth the thoughts of man.
Psalm 94:11 (KJV)

Fluffy's mind-reading ability is downright uncanny! I'm sure she must have ESP (extra-sensory perception)!

Many a morning I will let her outdoors while I'm getting breakfast and doing my morning chores. I leave the house at various times depending upon what errands and appointments are facing me for the day. And unless the weather is very good or the landlord is outside, I much prefer that Fluffy come inside until I return. Very seldom do I have to make an extra trip downstairs to find her, though, for which I am grateful, especially since arthritis hasn't made step climbing any easier! And just about the time I think I must locate Fluffy, she walks in the house of her own accord. Nor does she attempt to leave again when she sees me going out the door.

Another occasion when she seems to read my mind is bedtime. I'm an avid reader and usually relax in my La-Z-Boy with a good book before heading for bed. I can get out of the recliner to get a glass of ice tea or take some meat out of the freezer for the morrow, and Fluffy pays no attention.

But let me get out of that chair with the intention of picking her up and going to bed, and she gives a grunt and runs toward the bedroom, sneaking underneath the furniture far enough that I can't reach her! How does she know what I want? I've even tried doing several other things first before reaching for her, making several trips through the living room in the process. But she doesn't move a muscle—until I come into the room once again with the intention of snatching her off the floor before she knows what I'm doing. It never works! I hate to admit it, but at such times she outwits me mentally! I'm sure she must have cat ESP!

Thank You, Lord, because You know my thoughts afar off. May they always be pleasing in Your sight. And even as I am continually in Your thoughts, Father, may I keep You always in my thoughts, for Your Word says that You will then keep me in perfect peace.

Mine!

Don't think only of yourself. Try to think of the other fellow, too, and what is best for him.
I Corinthians 10:24 (TLB)

Fluffy has a catnip scratching box that she's enjoyed for several years. But when Shoe, her neighbor cat, discovered the fascinating box with its delightful catnip fragrance, Fluffy adopted a completely different attitude toward that pseudo scratching post. I don't know whether she learned it from Shoe, or not.

You see, after Shoe would sneak into the apartment, roll in the catnip and spread it all over the living room rug, she would then climb on top of the box—it was only about three inches off the floor—and hunker down on it for a snooze! Because Fluffy was so unhappy with Shoe in the house, I kept sending our unwelcome visitor home whenever I found her. Sometimes I'd carry her in my arms, sweet talking her so she wouldn't blame me for depriving her of her stolen catnip pleasure. Other times I would scold and stomp my feet in an effort to frighten her, not only so she'd go home, but also so she wouldn't return. It didn't work! That catnip attracted Shoe like the North Pole attracts a compass needle!

Then one day my two brain cells collided with each other and voila! A new idea was born! I'd make a catnip box for Shoe just like the one Fluffy had and put it on her own back porch. But Shoe ignored my completed project and continued her uninvited visits to our house to play with Fluffy's box.

That's when Fluffy started acting just like Shoe! (Now Shoe, you understand, was only about a year old, while Fluffy was supposed to be a mature cat at the ripe old age of eight!) Suddenly Fluffy began jumping on her box whether Shoe was around or not; but, unlike Shoe, she wouldn't sleep there. Instead, she would sit astride that box arrogantly like a Queen on her throne. Her expression, which needed no interpretation, shouted loudly and clearly for all the world to hear, "This box is mine, mine, mine!"

Shoe went to kitty heaven more than a year ago, and while Fluffy still enjoys getting "drunk" on catnip, she no longer manifests her spite by sitting atop her catnip box. Talk about green-eyed jealousy—well, I guess Fluffy's eyes really ARE green, come to think about it!

Father, You've told us in Your Word to take delight in honoring each other and to love each other with brotherly affection. Because I'm human, though, it's so easy to think of myself and my own needs first. Forgive me for my selfishness, and help me, I pray, to follow Your admonition and do everything I can to help others even as You would do if You were here on earth in person.

Much Ado About Nothing

A heart that manufactures wicked thoughts and plans.
Proverbs 6:18 (Amp)

Have you ever anticipated something bad that might happen? Have you ever thought of the worst possible outcome of a particular situation? Or have you ever let your imagination run away with you? If so, you're in good company—Fluffy's company, to be exact!

Fluffy's neighbor kitty, Shoe, used to sneak upstairs in our back attic whenever she could. And Fluffy had no use for Shoe—or any other cat, for that matter. But that didn't stop Shoe from seeking our hospitality any time she found our downstairs door ajar.

There was a footstool stored in the attic that Fluffy liked to sleep on, so one day I folded an old quilt and laid it on top which would give her a nice, soft bed whenever she felt like being alone—hopefully for her daily devotions. But Shoe decided that was also a good place for her to rest when she came over for her daily visits. And with that decision, a battle royal was on!

Before Fluffy would venture outside, she would cautiously creep out the kitchen door and warily search the attic before proceeding further. What hissing and spitting went on whenever she spied Shoe making herself comfortable on that foot stool, intruding on her territory! Fluffy became so paranoid on one occasion when I was accompanying her through the back attic in an effort to allay her fears, that without remembering to look and see whether Shoe was even there, she simply snarled and hissed as she passed the empty stool. When I burst into uncontrollable peals of laughter over her making much ado about nothing, she simply favored me with an aggrieved look and with a determined stride marched into the kitchen.

Father, how often I fail to properly investigate situations and find myself becoming prejudiced, thereby making mountains out of molehills. Keep me from letting my imagination take flight and thinking wrong thoughts or anticipating the worst scenario possible. Instead, be Thou the Lord of all my thoughts so that I will not find myself guilty of making much ado about nothing.

Naughty Girl

Being punished isn't enjoyable while it is happening.
Hebrews 12:10 (TLB)

As any good parent does, I occasionally find it necessary to discipline "my sweet, little darling!" That's usually after she bites me without provocation. Or if she jumps on a table or stand where I have stashed some papers I'm working with and scatters them to the four winds. Other times she pounces on a Chinese Checkers game board and happily chases the marbles across the floor and under the furniture! She especially likes bookmarks and paper clips. The smaller the item, the more she enjoys knocking it down and running after it.

At my shrill "No, Fluffy, No!" she'll skitter out of reach and into hiding unless I manage to reach her first. A slight tap on her head either with my hand or a newspaper accompanies my reproachful "Naughty Girl!" Please understand that I never strike her hard enough to injure or hurt her, though.

I would think that any cat with even a wee bit of intelligence would try to escape the wrath of an angry owner. But not Fluffy. Never have I seen her make the slightest attempt to avoid discipline when I occasionally manage to catch her.

Instead she lays her ears back, flattens herself on the floor, and takes whatever meager punishment I mete out. Does she have a guilty conscience? Is she remorseful? I suppose I'll never know. But I do know she straightens out her behavior, but fast—temporarily, that is!

Heavenly Father, I know there are times when You in love and mercy deem it best to discipline me even though I don't appreciate it at the time. Help me to see, Lord, that You are doing it for my benefit. I know You only discipline those Whom You love; and although it isn't pleasant, I thank You because I know that afterwards it will yield the peaceable fruit of righteousness.

Nighttime Antics

If ye do these things, ye shall never fall.
II Peter 1:10 (KJV)

One of Fluffy's favorite after-dark pastimes is to chase bugs attracted to the front porch by the bright living room lights beaming out a most inviting welcome. Things get pretty exciting when she jumps over the low retaining wall of our gently-sloping floor to the roof of the first-story porch some twenty inches beneath. She gambols at top speed from one end to the other as comfortable as if she were frolicking on solid ground. I never know from one minute to the next what portion of the roof she's on unless she reaches a white paw into the air in an effort to grab some unsuspecting insect.

The problem is how to persuade her to come inside when I'm ready for bed. For a while I could blackmail her with kitty treats; but it didn't take long for her to catch on to my wily scheme, and after that no amount of rustling the paper bag or shaking the container could coerce her to leave her play. Coaxing, wheedling, scolding—nothing worked. And if I reached over the edge with a yard stick, hoping to frighten her, she thought I was playing. I can empathize with parents sitting in the dark, waiting and agonizing untold hours for the return of their teenagers from that first date!

If I tried shining the flashlight into her eyes to blind her temporarily, she just chased the beam of light around the narrow ledge. Occasionally she would get so engrossed in catching her prey that she would tumble to the ground some ten or twelve feet below, but she always landed on her feet unharmed, as any good cat would do.

She never pulled such shenanigans, of course, unless it was around midnight and I was ready for bed. When she would fall—or jump (I'm really not sure which!), I'd wearily drag myself down the stairs, tiptoeing cautiously so as not to disturb my landlord and his wife who had already been in dreamland for a couple of hours. I'm not afraid of the dark, but the inky blackness of a country night without street lights or even friendly lights from neighbors' houses, as well as dense trees, which shut out the friendly twinkle of stars—all of this would cause uncontrollable shivers to cascade up and down my spine as strange shadows emerged from the faint beam of my dim flashlight. Added to that was the unpleasant dampness of the late night dew squishing through my toeless slippers as I crept through the grass.

But Fluffy would be waiting both expectantly and unrepentantly when I rounded that last corner, her eyes shining in the darkness like over-sized glass orbs. She would purr her thanks profusely while ignoring the ensuing scolding all the way upstairs. Then it was the mad, familiar dash, with Fluffy attaining speeds up to twenty-six miles an hour, to see who could reach the still-open front door first—Fluffy, to dash out again, or I, to close the screen door!

Thank You, Father, for Your protection in my life. Keep me from playing around the edges of anything of a questionable nature spiritually that could cause me to stumble and fall from Your tender grasp. And when I do make mistakes, pick me up in Your loving arms and set my feet on the solid rock once again.

No Invitation Required

Come unto me, all ye that labour and are heavy laden, and I will give you rest.
Matthew 11:28 (KJV)

If I know I'm going to be relaxing in my La-Z-Boy with a good book for an appreciable length of time, I'll hunt for Fluffy, pick her up and cuddle her on my lap. Other times, she'll jump on my lap of her own volition, not realizing I won't be sitting down for any significant length of time. Of course, I don't have the heart to disappoint her, so I usually pick up a book lying on the nearby credenza and read for a while whether I had intended to or not.

It isn't always convenient to have a cat on my lap, especially one that wants a lot of petting. But Fluffy won't take "No" for an answer. If I'm reading the newspaper and see her approaching, I try to discourage her by opening the paper and hiding behind it. But she's too smart to be fooled by that trick. She jumps on my lap, anyway, nuzzles the paper until she finds a loophole, then sticks her head under it and looks up at me as much as to say, "Aha, I've found you!" Of course, I let her stay.

But did you ever try to work a crossword puzzle using a cat as a prop to write on? Most of the time I lean to the right in a most awkward position and use the arm of my chair to do my writing. When I visit the chiropractor for biweekly adjustments, he keeps commenting, "Your right side is out of alignment today." I don't have nerve enough to tell him why!

But Fluffy knows she needs no invitation to sit in the comfort and shelter of my lap. She's welcome any time whether it's convenient or not. I love her too much to refuse.

Loving Heavenly Father, thank You because I need no special invitation to come to You. Your door is always open. I never have to worry about being turned away. You're never too busy to help me, and You always welcome me with arms of love outstretched just waiting to receive me.

No Mouser She!

But be ye doers of the word,
and not hearers only.
James 1:22 (KJV)

Whoever heard of a cat that refused to catch mice—other than Garfield, in the cartoons, that is! I thought that all cats were mousers until Fluffy enlightened me! Perhaps she doesn't care for light "mouse" work any more than I care for light "house" work!

Living in an older house, I've always had problems with mice—like the time some of my organ pedals lost their sound. I'll never forget how mortified I was when the repairman removed the back of the organ and showed me a mouse nest lined with felt from around the wires that connected to the pedals! He just laughed at my red face and said that was a common occurrence in colder weather, especially in older houses—that mice like the warmth generated by the motor, the fan, or whatever it is that organs have for intestines!

Then there was the first time I used the air conditioner in my car one summer day. When I turned it on, all kinds of lint, feathers and dust swirled from the vent into the car. I jumped out faster than I had jumped in, coughing, sputtering, and trying to brush the residue off my clothes. The guys at the garage had a good laugh when I took the car in for servicing. Again, it was a family of mice keeping warm throughout the winter months, using the underside of the floor carpeting to line their nest.

Now wouldn't you think having a cat around would put an end to all such disconcerting plights? Not if the cat's Fluffy! I still rely on my trusty D-Con, both inside and out.

Ben, my landlord, still laughs about the time Fluffy was staying with his wife and him while I was gone for a few days. She was napping on a kitchen chair when he heard a noise coming from beneath the sink. Suddenly a mouse ran out. Fluffy opened one sleepy eye long enough to watch that mouse scurry across the kitchen floor and out of sight, then stretched, yawned and went back to sleep, making no endeavor whatsoever to chase the unsuspecting rodent!

Apparently no one has ever told Fluffy that cats are supposed to be mousers! If they have, she's paid absolutely no attention to them.

Father, it's not enough for me just to know what Your Word says. I need to let it speak to my inner man and act upon it, so that it will bear fruit in my life, and I, in turn, can be a blessing to others. Help me never to be guilty of only hearing Your Word while, at the same time, ignoring Your instructions.

No Tail Pulling Allowed

Touch not the unclean thing.
II Corinthians 6:17 (KJV)

Very seldom does a night pass but what it finds me traipsing from the bed to the davenport for a while. There's just something about leaning against the back of the davenport at the same time I'm lying down that lulls me to sleep. After an hour or so, I get awake just enough to stumble back to bed where sleep enfolds me in its welcoming arms for the remainder of the night.

Fluffy, of course, follows me on those nightly vigils. Once I'm comfortably ensconced on the davenport, she begins her routine of jumping on my chest, soothing me with her quiet singing, then softly creeping to the empty space by my feet. Now and then, however, she likes to torment me by pacing back and forth in the narrow space between the davenport and the coffee table. On those occasions, she simply wants me to reach down, pick her up, and set her on my chest.

One night her constant prowling aggravated me, for I

knew she was perfectly capable of jumping up on my chest by herself. Too sleepy for games that evening, I grabbed her tail and hung on, thereby impeding her measured steps. "Me! Ow! I'm 'fur'- ious," she spat, and then, with a cry of outrage at such unexpected and outlandish treatment, she took off. All was quiet on the home front, so I figured she was in a "snit," had curled up on the La-Z-boy, and was probably fast asleep.

Groggily I turned over and draped my arm off the side of the davenport onto the floor. Still miffed by my earlier rough and unaccustomed manhandling of her tail, Fluffy was patiently waiting, paws outstretched as she lay on her back securely hidden beneath the davenport! Before I could comprehend what was happening, she grabbed my hand with all fours, then bit and scratched me voraciously before running across the room and leaping onto the recliner where she spent the rest of the night—even after I returned to the bedroom!

I carried the "love marks" she inflicted for weeks. But I learned my lesson well: Don't play with fire—oops, I mean, Don't play with Fluffy's tail!

Father, may I never be guilty of "playing with sin"; for You want a holy people, separate unto Yourself, who have not defiled themselves with the base things of this wicked earth. Help me not to touch the unclean things of this world nor have any fellowship with the works of darkness so prevalent all around me, but to keep my eyes fixed on You and the higher things of life.

Nothing But The Best

...(H)ow much more shall your Father which is in heaven give good things to them that ask him?
Matthew 7:11 (KJV)

As a coupon-wielding and price-comparison shopper, I used to check the grocery shelves carefully before buying whatever brand of cat food was on sale, using my coupons at every chance opportunity. Until the day the vet made the mistake of giving me a sample of a special, nutritionally-oriented cat food, that is. Fluffy gulped it down like a hyper-active child turned loose in a candy store. So of course, even though it did cost considerably more than the plain, ordinary kinds of cat food, I switched to that particular brand—after all, nothing was too good for "my baby."

But when she contracted an infection and had to be given an antibiotic twice daily for a while, the only way I could get her to take her medicine was to mix it with canned cat food. Again, nothing but the best would do for "my little darling," so I started buying Fancy Feast—the cheaper store-brand names would never be good enough! By the time

Fluffy was over her somewhat lengthy illness, she was hooked on that expensive canned stuff and I didn't have the heart to wean her away from it. I never went so far, though, as to dish it out on a genuine crystal goblet as some of the cat commercials portray, for I don't own any crystal ware!

But I have spent a considerable amount of money on toys for her only to have her refuse to play with them. You'd think she'd be considerate of my feelings and show some appreciation for my spending hard-earned cash for her happiness. Even at the end of a tight budget, I have, at times returned something of my own to the supermarket shelves in order to purchase a toy that I thought would delight her.

What it all boils down to, I guess, is that because I love to give her good things, I give her the best I can. After all, she's "my only child."

Thank You, Father, for giving me the best You have—Your only begotten Son. And thank You, too, for continuing to give me blessings and good things from your bounty on a daily basis. How I love You as I continue to acknowledge that every good and perfect gift comes from You.

“Now I Belong to Jesus”

...(W)e are [even here and] now God’s children.
I John 3:2 (Amp.)

I’m a single parent! In my wildest dreams, I never thought I’d have to make such a statement! It’s all because of Fluffy. I don’t know how many homes she had before she came to live with me. Although all her prior owners were allergic to her long hair, I wasn’t! The only thing I’ve ever been allergic to is men—that’s why I’m a single parent, even if my offspring is just a cat!

What a pleasure it had been to retire shortly before I inherited Fluffy. I enjoyed doing what I wanted to do when I wanted to do it. At long last I could travel whenever I desired for as long as I cared to. Having a cat in the house, however, changed all of that, and guilt suddenly set in whenever I’d make an overnight trip. After all, I had a responsibility to care for and protect any pet I might decide to adopt. My conscience refused to let me leave an animal alone in the house for days at a time, even with plenty of food and water. Pets are social creatures, too, and need proper companionship.

After mulling over the pros and cons of both sides of my situation, I decided to return Fluffy to her previous owners. Then I learned they were going to give her away again.

"To whom are you giving her?" I inquired one day.

"We don't know," they hesitated, shaking their heads. "We'll put an ad in the newspaper and find somebody to take her," they added, almost as an afterthought.

"And give her to just anyone?" I quizzed in a state of semi-shock. "How do you know what kind of family she'll have? What if they mistreat her?" I persisted, thoroughly alarmed at this turn of events.

"Oh, I'm a pretty good judge of character," replied the husband, smugly, as if that should allay any doubts and fears I might harbor.

"No, way," I made an instantaneous decision I've never regretted. "She's coming back with me."

And when I handed the veterinarian $200 a few weeks later in return for his services to "my adopted baby," I knew she was mine forever.

No wonder Fluffy likes to sing, "Now I belong to Lois," her version of a chorus she's often heard me sing, "Now I belong to Jesus."

Thank You, Father, that I'm Your child. I belong to You. Because You're my Father, I know You will always be with me and I will never have to worry about being alone, even if I am single. Thank You, too, for Your care and protection and for supplying all my needs. I'm so glad I'm Your responsibility.

Obedience

...(Y)ou have obeyed with all your heart.
Romans 6:17 (TLB)

Fluffy, for the most part, is an obedient cat. I can't say she's always "willingly" obedient, but she's obedient, nonetheless.

When evening shadows begin to stretch their bony fingers across the yard, I bring her in the house. Of course she prefers to stay outside to chase the many bugs and insects that appear at dusk. She follows close upon my heels like a dog fresh out of obedience school as I call her and we begin our nightly trek indoors. I remind her of all the neat things she can do inside such as go out in the front attic or on the front porch where she can still chase myriad creatures of the night. Then, at the foot of the stairs, she balks.

I could easily pick her up and carry her inside, but I enjoy her reaction when she decides to go against her will. All I do is sweet-talk her. "Come on, Fluffy; time to go in," I coax as I barely touch her hind legs. You'd think I was physically torturing her as she looks up at me and gives a most piteous "meow" before racing up the steps like a speeding arrow. But that pitiful meow says plainer than words, "I'll go, but I don't want to." Yet she loves me enough to obey!

Someone once said that it is not difficult to obey when you know the character of the individual you're obeying. Guess I'd better explain that to Fluffy, for apparently she's never read in her kitty Bible any instructions about obeying cheerfully from the heart.

Father, because You desire cheerful obedience from Your children, grant that my obedience might never be given to You grudgingly, but freely, from a heart of love and gratitude for all Your untold blessings to me.

Of Cats and Sparrows

Not one sparrow. . .can fall to the ground without your Father knowing it.
Matthew 10:29 (TLB)

Fluffy was sick!

For days prior she had been acting more like a young kitten rather than a sedate, nine-year-old feline. I've always said that she takes after her mother, and this was no exception. For as someone—two someones, in fact—told me last week on separate occasions, "Lois, you sure don't act your age!" In self-defense, I want to make it clear that was their response when they learned how old I was. "And how old is that?" you ask. Sorry, I wouldn't tell even if I knew! Fluffy wasn't acting her age, either!

As active and mischievous as she was the night before last, I wasn't prepared for her to be so listless yesterday morning. She wouldn't get up, she wouldn't purr, she wouldn't eat or drink, and she wouldn't use her kitty litter. (You heard about the police officer who arrested a cat for kitty litter, didn't you?) Fluffy didn't seem to be injured, and she wasn't lame when I finally persuaded her to take a couple steps. She wouldn't cry or flinch when I picked her up; but wherever and in whatever position I laid her down, she stayed like that for hours on end. I even brought her a small dish of strawberries with Cool Whip, which she dearly loves, but she turned her head.

I hesitated to take her to the vet as she doesn't like to ride in a car and cries constantly when in her cat carrier. *Is there anything I can do?* I pondered.

That's when I remembered the Scripture about the Lord seeing every little sparrow that falls. *How many sparrows annually would that be?* I speculated. *And if God cares that much for sparrows,* I reasoned, *wouldn't He also care for cats? After all, He did create them.* So I did the only thing I knew to do—I prayed!

It was 6:00 o'clock last evening when Fluffy walked through the apartment, went out on the front porch and jumped on the swing—the most I had seen her move around all day. By 8:00 o'clock I peeked out the door and saw her vigorously washing her face. In a few minutes she was her usual self, running and playing, tormenting me, eating and drinking and using her litter box!

Does it pay to pray, even for pets? I'll let you decide.

Thank You, Lord God, because there's nothing in my life too small to pray about. I know You love me; and because I love Fluffy and care for her, You are also concerned about that which belongs to me. And thank You, too, that when I came to You with my request boldly, you both heard and answered my petition.

Oh! The Pain!

Christ also suffered for us.
I Peter 2:21 (KJV)

The inevitable finally happened—I cut my finger opening a tin of cat food! I haven't always fed Fluffy canned food. For a while I purchased nutritionally-balanced dry morsels from the vet in 11-pound bags, two bags at a time. That would last several months. Price wise, I'm sure it must have been as expensive as those small cans of Fancy Feast that cost around 30 cents each! But that was the only kind of canned food the fussy animal would eat. That was OK with me since I didn't like the smell of leftover CANNED food, especially seafood varieties!

One day new neighbors moved in, along with three cats that quickly found their way uninvited to my upstairs apartment and to the dry food which I always left in plain sight for Fluffy to eat whenever she might be hungry. However, she became so upset with other felines invading her territory that she refused to go outdoors any more. Her piteous cries when the other cats sneaked into our house were heart wrenching. The only way I could alleviate the difficult situation was to keep all my doors tightly closed.

The remorse I suffered from denying Fluffy the privilege of going outside in the summertime had me pondering what I could do to make up for my cruelty of keeping her in the house all the time. I came up with the idea of appeasing my conscience by feeding her Fancy Feast—something she had had in the past only on special occasions such as Thanksgiving or Christmas. Each week my grocery cart was filled with small cans of fancy food—salmon, whitefish, turkey and giblets—any flavor but chicken. I couldn't bribe her to touch the chicken flavor even though she was crazy for the turkey and giblets. How she knew the difference I never could figure out. But what else would you expect of a cat who associates with a smart owner?

What a nuisance to open those tiny cans with the electric can opener. I was ecstatic when they finally added tabs whereby one could just rip the lids off—except I knew that sooner or later I'd cut my finger as I yanked on a tab to rip the lid back. Sure enough, that's what happened last week. It was just a small cut on the side of my finger, but it hurt worse than a bad paper cut even though I applied a soothing lotion. I was reminded of the pain every time my fingers touched something. Ever try working without having your fingers rub against each other?

I tried to get some sympathy from Fluffy, but she completely ignored my injured digit! Know what? I still love her just as much as ever in spite of the pain I endured just to placate her finicky palate. I told her so, too!

Father, don't ever let me forget the pain that Your Son Jesus endured for me when He died on the cruel cross of Calvary. And thank You, Jesus, for loving me so much that You were willing to withstand the pain that I deserved to bear.

Cat Trivia

FLUFFY ANSWERS YOUR MOST FREQUENTLY ASKED QUESTIONS

Q. Why does the water in a toilet bowl appeals to cats?
A. Because it's always cold and fresh.

Q. How much do cats sleep?
A. As much as 16-18 hours daily.

Q. Why do cats insist on kneading laundry fresh from the dryer?
A. It's in our genes; it's something we just can't resist.

Q. When cats nip each other during play, does it hurt?
A. No. Our skin is thicker than human skin and is covered by fur, so no damage is inflicted.

Q. Why do cats rub their cheeks against furniture or a person's leg?
A. This is their way of marking the object or person as their own by leaving a bit of their scent.

Q. How many sounds can a cat make?
A. 17 different sounds.

Q. How fast can a cat move?
A. When it makes a mad dash for something, it can attain speeds up to 31 miles per hour.

Q. Is it OK to feed my cats cold cat food kept in a refrigerator?
A. It will be easier for them to eat it if it is heated a little bit in the microwave.

Q. I've heard I should not feed my cat dog food. Why?
A. Because it lacks a substance that is crucial for a cat's eyesight.

Q. My cats don't seem to mind going outdoors in even the coldest of weather. Why?
A. Because their skin is insensitive to temperature except for their noses. But hey—don't leave them out very long at a time.

Q. Is it OK to feed my cat chocolate ice cream? She loves it.
A. No. Chocolate, and Tylenol, by the way, are both poisonous to cats.

Q. Why do cats bury their feces?
A. To cover their trails from predators.

Q. Other than helping control the pet population, is there any advantage in neutering a cat?
A. Yes. It can extend the life of a cat by two or three years.

One Mistreated Cat

For I am convinced that nothing
can ever separate us from his love.
Romans 8:39 (TLB)

Although Fluffy can hold her own in the hissing and spitting department when she gets riled up, she seldom turns her venom towards me—unless I tease her too much. My landlord tells her she has the best of two worlds, both at his house and mine, but sometimes she still thinks she's one mistreated cat.

She howls and yowls when I force her into her cat carrier, and then rattles the bars of the door in an effort to be released from her prison, but she doesn't hiss. Guess who holds her at the vet's while she undergoes an examination and gets her shots? But during this ordeal, her well-directed hissing and spitting is aimed toward the doctor, not me. During the summer months, I make her come inside prior to nightfall. She cries and sasses me something shamefully, but she doesn't hiss. I comb the snarls in her long fur as gently as I can, and although she attempts to jump off my lap and run away, she doesn't spit. When I try to wean her from canned cat food, after using it to get medicine down her little gullet, she looks at me so reproachfully that I almost lose my resolve; but she doesn't hiss and spit.

As I read over this list of my ill treatment of her, no wonder she thinks she's been abused! Poor thing.

But let me put her on her back and tickle her silky, white tummy too hard, and the hissing and spitting begin, together with biting and scratching! She sure knows how to administer revenge, swiftly and effectively!

On those few occasions, I simply bury my face in her tummy (she's never even attempted to attack my face) and tell her, "I love you anyway, Fluff." That simple declaration appeases her ruffled feelings and turns her hissing and spitting into the contented rumble of her purring mechanism.

Father, thank You because You love me in spite of any cross You may have called me to bear. Thank You, too, for the loving assurance You've given me that some day my cross will be exchanged for a victor's crown.

Only Fish in the Pond

And other sheep I have, which are not of this fold.
John 10:16 (KJV)

Fish, sheep, cats—do I have my metaphors mixed or what? All I know is that Fluffy thinks she should be the only fish in the pond—oops, I mean the only cat on the hillside. And she was, for many years, until new neighbors moved in some time ago.

You see, there are only two houses on our hilltop, and Fluffy had enjoyed the run of both premises all to herself barring any uninvited visitors which she quickly chased away with her nasty hissing and spitting. After all, the hilltop was her territory, and you needn't think she was going to share it with other felines.

The battle lines were drawn when the neighbors got a cat! *How nice it will be,* I hopelessly built an air castle in the beginning, *for Fluffy to have another cat for companionship.* But such was not to be the case—she made that clear the first time she laid eyes on her new four-legged neighbor. Nor did the situation improve when the neighbor cat presented her family with two new-born kittens some weeks later!

Those kittens were adorable. *Surely Fluffy's mothering instincts will take over, now,* I anticipated, *and she will accept the helpless, but cute little balls of fluff.* No way! Those kittens were too tiny to even know what they were supposed to do the first time she hunched her back, spitting and hissing at them with the venom of a rattlesnake ready to strike.

And did you ever try to teach a cat—big or little—to stay on its own premises when it saw its owner visiting the neighbors? The neighbors and I were friends from the first. As their cats grew, they would tag along whenever the children or their parents came over to my house. My cat would do the same when I went over to their house.

Although Fluffy would never attack her self-proclaimed enemies, she would hiss and spit and cry like a wounded animal each time she caught a glimpse of them. On one occasion, the emotional stress even caused her to get sick to her stomach!

The passing of time has brought changes, however. Mama kitty, next door, is now in kitty heaven. The little ones are grown and have left home as children sooner or later do. Once again, Fluffy is "Queen of the Hill," I mean the only fish in the pond—no, I'll get it right yet—she's the only cat on the hillside, proudly ruling her own territory.

Father, may I learn a lesson from Fluffy and remember that You have other children in addition to just those of my own little circle. Help me to put aside criticism, judgmentalism, and differences of opinion and accept as my brothers and sisters in the Lord those who have put their faith and trust in You, those who have received You as Lord and Savior.

Patience Personified

For when your patience is finally in full bloom, then you will be ready for anything.
James 1:4 (TLB)

Fluffy's overall attitude is, Que será, será!

She seldom meows to come inside when she is outdoors, in the attic, or on the front porch. Even in cold weather, she simply waits patiently until such time as I happen to miss her and remember to let her in. She does scold me, however, once I come to her rescue.

She reminds me of a friend who tells how he didn't talk until he was almost two years old for the simple reason he didn't need to talk. He had a one-word vocabulary that no one ever figured out how he picked up. If he wished to have something, all he had to do was say something that sounded like "Allure," and he automatically got whatever it was he desired at that particular time! Similarly, Fluffy just patiently sits in front of whatever she wants, whether it's an empty food dish, a litter box that needs cleaning, or a door to be opened. After all, any cat knows that if it sits and looks at a door long enough, it will open!

While I don't advocate her "Que será, será" attitude as a trademark for humans to embrace, I do envy her her patience! My only problem is that I want patience, and want it now! In fact, I want it yesterday!

Father, if there's one trait I need to develop, it's patience. Thank You for Your forbearance and longsuffering with my slowness to learn not only this but also other lessons that You see I need to master. Thank You, also, for the rough places in my life, for I know that they, too, will cause my patience to grow until I can become strong in character, full and complete in You.

Perfect Faith

Even though the fig trees are all destroyed, and there is neither blossom nor fruit. . .yet I will rejoice in the Lord.
Habakkuk 3:17, 18 (TLB)

It's such a temptation to tease Fluffy. She's so good natured, that it's only occasionally I've gone too far with my teasing and have experienced her sharp, vindictive teeth and claws in retaliation!

I like to tickle her nose with her tail; she never objects. I like to fold and unfold her soft front paws when she's on my lap sleeping; she pays no attention. I've been known to take her front feet and try to dig a hole in her kitty litter, just to help her, you know; she doesn't object—nor does that speed up the process! I've poked her nose in a bowl of milk when I thought it was time she should drink more liquid; but if she's not thirsty, she throws her head back disdainfully and marches to another part of the house. When she tries to sleep, I sometimes decide I can find a more comfortable position for her. I'll stretch her out like a wiener dog, and she continues her snooze without interruption. Or I'll curl her up into a snail-like ball; she just buries her head under her paws further still and sleeps on contentedly.

Fluffy's version of Habakkuk 3:17, 18 apparently reads, "Even though Lois teases and torments me, and ties me into knots, yet I will trust in her, for I know she will never deliberately hurt me."

I've often made the statement—somewhat of an exaggeration, I must admit in all honesty—that I can twist Fluffy into a pretzel and she won't object. At the same time I can only shake my head and murmur, "What faith! What trust!"

How I envy her!

Or is envy a sin?

Father, I admit my faith and trust in You at all times and under all circumstances is sometimes lacking, and I'm truly embarrassed that a cat can display those same qualities so much more easily than I, especially since the object of my faith is not another human being, but You, my God and my Savior! Forgive me, Lord, for my doubts and unbelief. Remove my fear and distrust, and through Thy rich grace impart strength to my fainting heart.

Picky Diner

...(F)eed me with food convenient for me.
Proverbs 30:8 (KJV)

Because I'm a product of depression years, I'm somewhat of a fanatic when it comes to wasting food. Those were the days, you know, when we were told, as youngsters, to eat everything on our plates because of the starving children overseas. No one ever explained, though, how our eating everything in sight would actually help those destitute little ones in foreign lands. Nevertheless, the underlying principle of "waste not, want not" has always been a guiding factor in my life—and today that precept applies to even Fluffy!

If I share a few pieces of chicken, or ham, or bacon with her and she walks away without eating it all, I'm not about to throw the remaining bits in the garbage. Trying to reason with her about cats who have to forage for their own food doesn't phase her. Even tales about starving cats in the world fall on deaf ears. So I try the next best thing by mixing and hiding her leftovers in her regular cat food. Sometimes that works, and sometimes it doesn't! When all else fails, though, I can open a can of "people" tuna and pour the juice over her food—that always works! By one means or another,

I'm going to see to it that she doesn't waste food—not even one single bite! For it's my responsibility to see that she's fed what she needs!

Father, how many times I refuse to accept the spiritual food You desire to feed me and turn away from some truth in Your Word that You see I really need. But how faithful and patient You are as You present Your rules and laws and principles to me in first one way and another—perhaps through a song, a testimony, a Bible study or Sunday School lesson, or a message. And thank You that eventually I "eat and digest" the precepts You see I need and desire to impart to me.

Professional Mime

You ought to follow our example.
II Thessalonians 3:7 (TLB)

One summer when Fluffy was sick and the vet was unable to pinpoint the cause of her illness, I myself was reacting to a new medication which my physician had prescribed for me. I don't know which of us was the sicker, Fluffy or me! We seemed to go in cycles, however; if she was under the weather, I was feeling better. When I got worse, she snapped out of her molly-grubs. Only occasionally were both of us not "up to snuff" at the same time. On those days, I lay on the davenport, getting up only for a drink, a bit of food, or to use my kitty litter. Ditto for Fluffy!

Several weeks after both of us had put our troubles behind us, a friend asked me how I had felt during my illness. After I described my symptoms, she further questioned if Fluffy had acted the same way. I was astonished; I had never thought of any connection between the two of us as we battled our maladies. Then I remembered that so many times I had remarked to Fluffy, "You act the way I feel!"

Can cats actually take on the characteristics of their owners when they're sick? My friend assured me that had happened with a cat belonging to an uncle of hers. And, of course, I'd heard of cats that had lost their owners through death and who, in turn, had pined away themselves because of their great grief.

I reflected on the trauma that Fluffy and I had gone through the preceding weeks. Sure enough, it was just after my doctor changed my medicine and the side effects began to appear that Fluffy became sick. When I put myself in the care of a new physician who quickly changed my medication, it didn't take long for me to bounce back to health. And that's when Fluffy also made a permanent recovery!

Coincidence? I'll never know. But this I do know—I'm careful what kind of example I set before her these days. Now I don't even let her know when I have a headache!

Thank You, Jesus, for the example You set before Your followers when You walked on earth among men, an example that is safe for Your children to follow even today. Help me always to follow in Your footsteps for I know that nothing can harm me so long as I let You lead the way.

Pur-r-rfect

Herein is our love made perfect.
I John 4:17 (KJV)

Every time I enter my bathroom, my eyes fall on a sampler that Willie (my landlady) gave me as a Christmas present years ago. Painstakingly she had cross stitched the profiles of two cats, one on either side of the words, "Cat lovers are Pur-r-rfect." Her tasteful choice of yellow lettering on an off-white background matches my color scheme "pur-r-rfectly." It also matches Fluffy's coloring "pur-r-rfectly."

Fluffy reads that sampler, too, every time she follows me in to my kitty litter. Apparently she knows how to read; and now, whenever she's naughty, she tilts her little head to one side and purrs, "After all, nobody's pur-r-rfect!"

And doting mother that I am, I happen to think I have a "pur-r-rfectly" wonderful cat—most of the time, anyway! In return, Fluffy seems to think she has a "pur-r-rfectly" marvelous mother. I know I'm prejudiced, but I wholeheartedly agree with her sentiments! If you question my sanity or get the impression I'm boastful in this respect, I would have to admit you're right.

As the Apostle Paul said, however, I'm not boasting of my own works; my boast is in the Lord. It is He, through the blessed Holy Spirit, Who turns even my weaknesses into "pur-r-rfection." If you doubt my claims, I would challenge you to get a good concordance and study the Scripture references for words such as "boast," "complete," and above all, "perfect!" (Just be sure to use the correct spelling of "perfect" when you do!)

Yes, I'd say Fluffy and I love each other with a "pur-r-rfect" love. How "pur-r-rfect" are you?

Thank You, Father, because I don't have to struggle in my own strength to achieve the perfection You demand of Your children—heart perfection, inner perfection. Thank You for Your Holy Spirit Who makes me complete through Christ Jesus. Thank You, too, because You never require me to do or be anything that's impossible, but will, in all situations, help me fulfill Your desires for my life.

Scarred For Life

...(H)e showed them his hands and side.
John 20:20 (TLB)

Our quarter-acre lot abounds with thorny shrubs of all kinds—barberry bushes, wild roses, raspberries, blackberries and holly plants, to name a few. Of course, when Fluffy came to live with me, she had to snoop around until she found them all.

The first two or three summers I had her, those thorns attracted her the way molasses attracts flies. Her favorite pastime those days, next to rolling over uneven floor boards and coarse cement porches, was brushing her nose against prickly thorns and rough tree bark! It wasn't long until her sensitive white nose was no longer white, for she rubbed until splotches of both fur and skin disappeared and her nose was one speckled, bloody mess. Still she continued to rub, opening the scabs that were trying to form, making even bigger and deeper wounds!

At first I couldn't figure out what was causing her nose to be so disfigured. It took several days of following her around the yard, sneaking up on her unexpectedly! Being fair-skinned, myself, I knew that excessive sun would bring out the freckles—I have enough to prove it! But it was more than sun that was causing Fluffy's disfigurement! How embarrassing it was to explain her condition to the vet when I took her for her annual checkup and rabies shot in August; for as soon as he glimpsed her pock-marked nose, he assumed I had brought her in for treatment of an allergy of some kind. By the third summer, however, he remembered and laughed at her appearance.

I lost count of the number of cans of cat repellent I purchased those years as the mornings found me settling into a routine of walking around the estate and spraying anything that boasted thorns! Even that didn't eliminate the problem completely, just lessened it somewhat!

My "four-footed baby" reminds me of a silly couplet I once read to the effect that if one keeps his nose to the grindstone long enough, all that's left is himself, the grindstone and his bloody nose!

The last few years Fluffy has somehow lost interest in thorn bushes, for which I'm most grateful. And while her nose is no longer bloody, she will, however, carry her pock-marked scars to the grave!

Thank You, Lord Jesus, for Your precious nail-scarred hands that point the way to redemption for all who will put their faith and trust in You. Thank You for Your blood that was shed on Calvary on my behalf, and for the scars You so willingly bore for me.

Seafood Diet

I am my body's sternest master.
I Corinthians 9:27 (J.B. Phillips)

Why do cats have sense enough to quit eating once their little tummies are full? Fluffy has cat food at her disposal twenty-four hours a day. Her dishes always have food in them; many times she even has a side dish of turkey available. But somehow, she has sense enough to listen to the signals her brain sends her and stop eating when she's full—even when her beloved turkey is served!

When I first got Fluffy, I watched her to see if she would try to sample the D-Con that I've habitually placed in strategic locations for our nighttime visitors that she's never shown an interest in catching. Not once did she try to eat it. Who told her that D-Con is poisonous? Sometimes I think that cat's got more sense than I have!

Wonder if Ponderosa—my favorite eating place—would let me bring Fluffy along the next time I eat out? Perhaps I could learn some lessons from her about not feeling guilty if I don't eat every morsel on my plate. It's so embarrassing when it takes both the manager and a waitress to pry me out of my booth and help me into the car! (Not that this has ever actually happened—yet!)

And talk about poison—how I love it! Especially when it's chocolate—chocolate of any kind. Nuts, of course, help disguise the poisonous sugar and caffeine. Almonds are my favorite nuts because they're on my diet. Diet? What diet? The seafood diet, of course—when I see food, I eat it.

Well, that double chocolate fudge ice cream is calling me–oops, I almost forgot. Ice cream's not on my diet!

Father, Your Word tells me very plainly that my body is the temple of the Holy Ghost. You've also given me plenty of instructions for disciplining and caring for this body that is made in Your image. I want to be at my best to fulfill Your plan for my life and be of service to You and my fellow men. Therefore, help me always to have the strength to practice moderation in all things, and that includes my eating habits!

Seventy Times Seven

Lord, how oft shall my brother sin against me, and I forgive him? Till seven times?
Matthew 18:21 (KJV)

O Lord, you are so good and kind, so ready to forgive.
Psalm 86:5 (TLB)

Fluffy fights her annual trips to the vet from beginning to end. It's a struggle to get her in her cat carrier before we leave home. She scolds and cries and rattles the prison bars of her carrier all the way there and back. She hisses and growls at both doctors and aides even though I am holding her, petting her and whispering sweet nothings into her ears.

And what a guilt complex I endured the one time it was necessary to hospitalize her overnight! I figured she'd have nothing to do with me when I picked her up the next day. In fact, I felt so sorry for her that I didn't put her in her carrier for the return trip to more familiar surroundings. To my surprise, she lay on the front seat beside me with her head in my lap all the way home!

But all is forgiven once she sets her dainty feet on her home territory. She climbs on my lap at the first opportunity and throws her little "buzz saw" into high gear as she sings her thanks to me for rescuing her from a dreadful nightmare. I, too, breathe a sigh of relief as I realize that everything's forgiven and forgotten.

How thankful I am that she harbors no grudge, bears no malice, and keeps no record of the number of times this scenario has been repeated. Apparently she's learned the secret that Christ taught Peter—that of forgiving seventy times seven.

Heavenly Father, thank You for being so good and kind, so ready to pardon regardless of the number of times I find it necessary to seek Your forgiveness. Instill within me that same Christ-like attitude of forgiveness toward others, as I recall Your exhortation to forgive even as I would also be forgiven by You.

Sharpening Those Claws

Be ready always to give an answer.
I Peter 3:15 (KJV)

I don't believe I could ever have a cat declawed. Fluffy, however, had her front paws declawed by a previous owner. But she surely knows how to make up for her loss by scratching with her hind feet to say nothing of substituting her teeth for those front claws! She has adapted her sharp teeth to the specific job of stabbing and slicing with the precision of a surgeon, thus leaving wounds similar to those of a claw scratch.

Declawing her, however, did not eliminate her natural instinct to sharpen the missing talons. By now, my La-Z-Boy would be in shreds if she did own front claws. I've never tried to break her of the habit since I know that her attempt at sharpening claws which she doesn't have can't ruin the furniture, and also since the recliner is the only thing she seems attracted to for that particular pastime.

Whenever I see Fluffy stretching and digging fast and furiously, I simply laugh and ask, "Are you sharpening those claws you don't have again?" Apparently she feels the need to be prepared and blissfully continues her harmless occupation.

I, too, like to be prepared, especially when it comes to answering questions or defending myself in any given circumstance. After all, Scripture does tell us to be ready to give an answer to those who might ask us about our beliefs. Somewhere down through the years, though, I'm afraid I've gone too far with that concept; and in my mind I will play possible scenarios over and over. *If this happens, I'll say this.* Or *if so-and-so says thus-and-so, I'll respond like this.* And more times than I care to admit, what I'd say and do isn't exactly proper conduct for a Christian.

Like Fluffy trying to sharpen claws she doesn't have, I'm attempting to resolve situations that never happen. And I'm wasting precious energy that could be channeled more profitably in other endeavors.

Father, as You have promised in Your Word, I ask You to give me the right words whenever I'm called upon to witness to my faith. Help me, too, to tear down the evil imaginations of my natural mind, thus closing the door to the enemy so that he cannot sap my strength with wrong attitudes that would so easily take over my heart and mind.

Short Memory

Remember ye not the former things.
Isaiah 43:18 (KJV)

Like many humans, Fluffy has a good memory when she wants to, but she also has a short memory when it's convenient! (Do cats ever contract Alzheimer's?)

There's Dan—a friend who lives about a hundred miles from here but who, because of work and family responsibilities, is able to visit us only once every several years or so. Does Fluffy remember him? You bet she does, and torments him when she sees him until he pets her to her satisfaction! Does she recollect her annual trips to the veterinarian? You bet she does, and expresses her displeasure the moment I put her in the car!

In spite of her confinement during the winter months, last Spring it didn't take her long to recall that the new neighbors had a mother cat and two kittens who loved to visit us whenever they could sneak in unawares. Every time I tried to get Fluffy outside, she would cautiously creep out the kitchen door, belly almost dragging the floor, and check to see that there were no unwanted cats hiding in the attic. When she felt the coast was clear, she would cross the attic to her next stop—the top of the stairs. If no foreign kitty faces appeared, she would proceed to the first landing and peer around the corner prudently. Whenever she was outdoors, she would keep one wary eye on the lookout for kitty imposters as she prowled around what used to be her territory and hers alone.

Things have changed this summer, however, as the kittens finally struck out on their own after their mama went to "kitty heaven." And how quickly Fluffy has forgotten. No longer does she exhibit her former cautiousness, but races downstairs and roams the hilltop to her heart's content. However, I was surprised when she marched right over to the neighbor's back door the other day and wanted inside. Apparently she remembered that the former neighbors, from several years ago, used to let her in and feed her just inside the door! She forgot, or perhaps doesn't know, that two new kitties—house kitties, however—live there now.

Like her owner, Fluffy's memory sometimes fails her!

Father, help me to forget the sins and mistakes of my past that are under the precious blood of Your Son, the Lord Jesus Christ. May I, instead, remember with praise and thanksgiving the sacrifice He made and the great price He paid for my redemption. And may I never forget Your marvelous love for me, and the many blessings that You shower upon me from day to day.

Cat Trivia

KOMMENTS OVERHEARD BY FLUFFY AT A KAT KONVENTION

Mouser: My neighbor's human actually sets a place at the dinner table for her cat!

Carmel: My human rented her apartment just because it had a nice hideaway for my litter box!

Blackie: My human meows so well she confuses me, and I think another cat has come in the house!

Goldie: I've learned it's best for me to appear remorseful when I'm scolded.

Toby: My human claims she chooses her friends on the basis of how well I like them!

Callie: I find I can wiggle out of almost any trouble if I just purr and look cute.

Furry: When one of the humans in our town walks her cat, they wear matching outfits!

Ebenezer: I've finally learned that curtains are the easiest and fastest way to climb to the top!

Cleopatra: My human calls home from work and leaves messages on her answering machine for me!

Rascal: My favorite trick when my human catches me doing something naughty is to run under the bed so she can't reach me. It works every time!

Tiger: My humans have the towels in their bathroom marked "His," "Hers," and "Kat."

Malty: One thing I learned the hard way this year is that it's not safe to jump up on a garbage can with a hinged lid!

Whiskers: Have you ever noticed that cat owners don't know how to talk with non-cat people?

Malty: I can top all your stories. When my human's husband told her "Me or the cat," she never hesitated. Now it's just the two of us, although once in a while she admits she misses her husband now and then.

Signing Checks

And it is he who will supply all your needs.
Philippians 4:19 (TLB)

Fluffy was sick—had been for weeks. The vet couldn't find anything wrong with her; blood tests were fine; but shots and antibiotics only worked for a couple of weeks. Overnight hospitalization didn't provide any clues, either. Naturally I was upset when the vet told me plainly, "I don't know what's wrong with her."

I'm retired and on a limited income. And the services of vets, I found out, are not cheap. Why, I can go to my own doctor for far less money than I shell out to the vet for just one trip for Fluffy! And my prescriptions are much cheaper, too! But then, I guess Congress hasn't passed legislation, yet, authorizing Medicare for cats! And I'm very sure they're not covered under AARP, either. Wonder whether it would be wise to apply to EPIC for help with her prescriptions?

By the third time within two months that I had to write a check to the animal clinic, my nerves were shattered. Fluffy's frantic cries from the confinement of her hated cat carrier only increased my agitation. I quickly wrote out the check as fast as my shaking hand could move and handed it to the receptionist who tried to hide a smile as she gave a judicious cough before saying anything.

"Are you sure this is right?" she asked cautiously.

Dumbfounded at her question I looked at the check. It was signed: Fluffy!

Father, just as Fluffy depends upon me to "sign her checks" and provide for all her needs, so I depend upon You to supply all my needs according to Your riches in glory in Christ Jesus. Thank You because You never fail, and thank You because Your checkbook never runs out of funds.

Sitting At His Feet

Mary. . .sat at Jesus' feet.
Luke 10:39 (KJV)

Fluffy has this idea that I'm not capable of using my computer without her help. As much as I hate to admit it, sometimes I think she's right! During the day, she is content to jump up on the sewing machine, which is in the same room as the computer, and take a sun bath. In the evenings, though, she parks herself in a strategic spot around the corner from my computer desk and on the bedroom rug. That way she can see what's going on not only in the bedroom, but also in the living room as well as the computer room. Smart cat! (They say cats do take on the characteristics of their owners!)

Lately, though, she has been sneaking behind my computer desk and curling up amongst all the computer cords. I don't even know where half of those cords belong! Cords to the CPU, cords to the speakers, cords to the modem, cords to the printer, the keyboard, the monitor—cords, cords, cords. What would I do if she ever pulled one of them out of its socket?

Last week I purchased a nice, soft office chair that

swivels and has adjustable arms, back, and seat. As old age (ouch!) and scoliosis have combined to shorten my stature, I have the seat pumped up as high as I can get it—and it certainly makes reaching the keyboard easier! Just one minor problem, however—my feet won't touch the floor! Oh, well! One can't have everything, I guess! So I just prop my feet on the swivel part of the chair and swivel away to my heart's content—just like a professional executive!

Fluffy evidently approves of my new chair; for she has suddenly left her nest among the computer cords and now curls up right at my feet. I'm reminded of that every once in awhile when I stretch my feet and accidentally bump into her. Of course she responds with a none-too-polite grunt just to remind me of her presence.

It makes me think of an old, old hymn:

Sitting at the feet of Jesus,
O what words I hear Him say!
Happy place! so near, so precious!
May it find me there each day.

Jesus, may I set aside time each day to sit at Your feet and be blessed as I gaze upon Your face, as I gather grace and comfort from Your love, as I lay my sins and sorrows before You, and as I find rest, sweet rest just by being in Your presence, sitting at Your feet.

Snarls and Tangles

...(A)fterwards we can see the result.
Heb. 12:11 (TLB)

Fluffy likes attention. What else is new? Don't most cats? Most of all, she likes to have her long hair brushed. I've often thought I'd like to see just how long she'd let me brush her if I wouldn't stop. It's so tempting, especially since she purrs so loudly; but so far, she's won every round! Never once has she jumped off my lap when I brush her, which is about every other day—every day, in fact, when she starts to shed!

She never jumped off my lap, that is, until I bought another brush. You see, it was priced at only a quarter when I stopped at a yard sale on the spur of the moment one day. It had the nicest plastic bristles with multi-colored rounded ends. Perfect, I thought! That old brush I inherited when Fluffy came to live with me had wire bristles that were all bent out of shape. A change was definitely in order!

The first time I ran that new plastic brush through her thick orange coat, my eyes opened wide in surprise at the amount of loose hair it garnered. Next I tried it on the white patch of fur that graces her neck much like a collar. Same result. Great! At last I had discovered the secret of helping her shed what surely must be a hot, uncomfortable coat of hair during the heat of summer. I was sure this new brush was the perfect remedy for preventing all those tangles and snarls that I had to actually cut out with the scissors. Fluffy was so soft after she was groomed. She felt so cuddly when I would bury my face in her silky coat!

I had asked the vet one time if there was an easy way to eliminate the matted hair; and, if not, what was the best procedure to at least smooth it out. "Nothing to it," he boasted confidently, as he reached for a comb and ran it through a thick clump of Fluffy's knotted fur. That did it! The skirmish was on and Fluffy, of course, won! I choked back the laugh that involuntarily rose to my throat as the doctor grabbed for some antiseptic and a band-aid! Funny thing—I was holding her at the time, but she didn't try to bite me; she was after the nasty man with the nasty comb!

Her snarls and tangles still pose a problem. Smart cat that Fluffy is (takes after her owner, of course—I've never doubted that!), three or four swipes with that new plastic brush are enough, and off my lap she jumps! I do my best to coax her back, telling her how soft and silky she would be if she would only submit to that new brush. "Never mind the results," she meows, "just use my old, comfortable wire brush." Ever since then, she's kept her beady little eyes trained on those brushes and will have nothing to do with the one that is more effective.

Lord, how often I am just like Fluffy when You show me an area of my life that needs to be changed. Discipline is never enjoyable when it is happening—it hurts and I'm tempted to resent it. But help me, Father, to submit to Your loving ministrations of correction, knowing that afterwards the result will be a quiet growth in grace and character that will reflect Your Divine personality of love.

Songs in the Night

...God. . .gives songs in the night.
Job 35:10 (TLB)

I never found it necessary to close my piano keyboard until the night Fluffy decided to play a song at midnight! The organ, of course, can't be played unless it is turned on, and so far that's a trick she hasn't learned.

But the piano fascinates her. I thought perhaps the tones, especially on the treble keys, would be annoying to her sensitive ear. But whenever I sit down and tickle the ivories, she emerges from wherever she is and comes to lie next to the piano on the carpet, intently watching my fingers moving across the keys. (I haven't tried teaching her to read notes, yet; that's on my agenda for her future education!)

Several years ago she apparently decided that if my fingers could produce music, so could her paws. But she waited, of course, until the household was sound asleep before trying her skill. The "household" includes Ben and Willie, my landlord and his wife, who live downstairs.

Ben and Willie have often told me about the time that a former tenant in my apartment used to do her laundry in the middle of the night, and of course, they could hear the sound of the running water as she filled and emptied her washer. They didn't say anything, they claim, until she decided to vacuum the living room at 4:00 a.m. Then they said their piece and expressed their displeasure at being so rudely awakened at such an unearthly hour! So I've always been careful not to do anything that would disturb their rest after they've retired for the night. But apparently I neglected to mention that fact to Fluffy, and she wasn't too considerate of their need for "shut eye."

I awoke from a deep sleep one night, startled to hear someone playing the piano. *Had an intruder entered the house?* I wondered. *If so, how? And why would anyone choose to announce his or her presence with a piano concert?* Then I realized it wasn't an uninvited guest, but Fluffy, strutting her stuff on the keyboard as she hit every one of the eighty-eight keys! It was "mew-sic" to her ears!

When I asked Ben and Willie the next day how they liked their midnight concert, they assured me they hadn't heard it even though our bedroom windows had been open! The best part of it is that Fluffy evidently realized that "tinkling the ivories" just wasn't her forte, for she hasn't tried playing songs in the night since—even if the keyboard is left uncovered!!

Thank You, Father, for giving me Your songs in the night. When my mind is quiet and relaxed in the midnight hours, it seems I am more receptive to Your precious Holy Spirit as I lie awake thinking of You and how You've helped me. Truly I rejoice through the night beneath the shadow of Your wings (Psalm 63: 6, 7 LB).

Submission—Price Tag of Happiness

Submit yourselves therefore to God.
James 4:7 (KJV)

I don't suppose that Fluffy, being a cat, will ever give up wanting to do things her way. In fact, I don't think I ever knew a cat that didn't have a mind of its own. People, too (myself included), for that matter!

I can beg Fluffy to jump on my lap; but if she doesn't want to, she won't. As little as thirty seconds later, however, with a leap and a bound she plops into my lap. But by then, it is her idea—not mine! Sometimes I'll try to get her to go out in the front hallway, especially in winter time when it's too cold to be outdoors. As a rule, she enjoys prowling around the many and sundry boxes and bags stored there. I suppose it's a sneaky thing to do, but if I'm going to eat something I know she'll want, that front hallway is as good a place as any to send her for a while so she won't pester me to share my food with her. After all, she doesn't share her food with me; and sharing, I tell her, is a two-way street—although she doesn't seem to comprehend that. So I open the front door, beg, wheedle, and coax, but she just looks the other way. However, let me get comfortably settled in my recliner and she trots to the front door with a plaintive "meow." Now it's her idea to go out and she's more than willing!

In all honesty, though, I'll have to admit I have no trouble in getting her to come back in whenever I call. Now that's not saying she wants to. Invariably she'll utter a protesting "meow" or two, but without fail she obediently obeys my command. She soon forgets her reluctance, of course, when she is rewarded by a snack of one kind or another, usually a kitty treat! Other times my assurance that she's a good kitty, a good girl, and a good baby satisfies her. Or perhaps I'll pick her up and cuddle her for a few minutes. She's happy and is all smiles—I mean purrs—by that time.

Yes, happiness has its price tag. It means giving up her will for my will. But in the long run, it pays good dividends.

Hm-m-m! Is there a lesson there I should be learning?

Father, there are still times in my spiritual walk that I want to do my own thing, in my own way and in my own timing even though I know that the only way I can achieve true happiness is to submit to Your kind and holy will in all things. May I ever remember that You are too good to make a mistake and too loving to be unkind.

Talking Turkey

Be strong! Be courageous! Do not be afraid of them!
Deuteronomy 31:6 (TLB)

Fluffy spends a great deal of her outdoors time lying on my landlord's kitchen porch downstairs, for she can survey a lot of territory from that vantage point. She can check on all vehicles that come to either of the two houses on the hilltop, and she knows when they take their leave! That's also where she waits for me to return from running errands; the minute I turn in the drive, she heads for my parking space beneath the chestnut tree. Sometimes, though, she sees more than she is expecting.

I had been gone for several days and Fluffy was staying with Ben and Willie, my landlord and his wife. Ben told me the story when I got home. Fluffy was contentedly viewing her world from that kitchen porch when an unusual noise startled her from her peaceful reverie. Her eyes widened into two saucer-like orbs and her ears laid back flat on her head as a wild turkey flew down from nowhere and landed on the grass just a few feet in front of her. She had never seen a turkey before—a real, live one, that is. Before she could adjust to the strange sight, a second turkey landed, then a third, and a fourth until there were sixteen toms—"jakes," Ben called them—clustered in the front yard.

Fright filled Fluffy's body as she scrunched herself down on the porch smaller and smaller (her concept of becoming invisible) until she was not much bigger than a mouse—the coward! No way was she going to tackle such a formidable spectacle, even if the turkeys had invaded her territory and were also one of her favorite foods!

A few days later, though, when Ben asked if I wanted to taste some wild turkey, I couldn't help but wonder, hm-m-m-m-m! He hadn't been "buffaloed" by those turkeys. No, sir-e-e-e!

Thank You, Father, that I can depend upon You to confront all my enemies, that I don't have to face them in my own strength, which is inadequate. I never need be afraid because You're always there when I need You and will help me fight my battles when I put my trust in You.

The Best of Two Worlds

He shall receive. . .now. . .and in the world to come.
Mark 10:30 (KJV)

I was downstairs visiting with my landlord and his wife at the close of a perfect Spring day. Fluffy was nearby, chasing anything that moved. Occasionally she would rest contentedly on the cool cement porch; then again she would meander, uninvited, through the open door and make herself at home in Willie's kitchen.

"Fluffy," I scolded, "did you ask to go inside?"

"Let her alone," chided Ben. "She's all right and not hurting a thing. She's got the best of two worlds. Let her enjoy it."

Truer words were never spoken. Naturally she has the run of my second-floor apartment which includes a large front hallway, a back attic, and a third-floor cupola and attic. That should be enough to satisfy any cat's curiosity, but she also makes herself at home downstairs at Ben and Willie's. Whether it's cool weather or hot, she'll plaintively cry at their back door. When they obligingly respond to her demanding cry and let her in, she completely ignores them, walks across the kitchen floor and begs them to open the door and let her out onto the front porch on the opposite side of the house.

But when I go hunting for her, how do I get to the front yard? Through Ben and Willie's kitchen? Oh, no! I walk all the way around the house even in inclement weather, through rain and snow, before I find her. She comes running right away, but unless I pick her up and carry her, once again she meows at their side door, crosses through their kitchen, and waits for me at the back porch—her feet clean and dry while mine—forget it! Did I say she was smart like her owner? I sometimes think she's smarter than her owner although I'd never admit it—to her, anyway.

No wonder Ben thinks she has the best of two worlds!

But she's not the only one who can make that boast. As a child of God, I, too, have the best of two worlds, both in this present world and in the world to come.

Thank You, Heavenly Father, not only for Your love, Your goodness, Your mercy, and Your manifold blessings which I enjoy in this life, but also for the hope of the future—life everlasting in Your sacred Presence in a glorious mansion You've prepared for me on High.

The Green-Eyed Monster

...(J)ealousy is cruel as the grave.
Song of Solomon 8:6 (KJV)

Fluffy has green eyes—in more ways than one! She's jealous of the telephone! Our telephone (notice I say "our") sits on a stand next to "our" La-Z-Boy. And when that phone rings, Fluffy jumps off my lap and pouts!

It's not the noise she dislikes, for she can be on the floor and doesn't so much as flinch when it rings. The fire siren, just a half block away, can summon the volunteer firemen in its shrill tones, and she ignores it. The eighteen-wheelers can gun their engines as they roar up the hill at the side of our house, and she doesn't twitch a whisker. So I know it's not the noise of the telephone that frightens her and causes her to jump off my lap when the phone rings.

The only logical conclusion for her action under the circumstances is jealousy, green-eyed jealousy. For if I can't give her my undivided attention and have to talk to an inanimate object instead of to her, she'll let me know about it. Her actions shout more loudly than words, "If that's the way you want it, go ahead. I'm leaving!"

Father, it's so easy to become suspicious and distrusting of others, always imagining the worst. Help me to guard against harboring resentment or ill will toward my brothers and sisters in the Lord. Instead, may I always manifest Your attitude of love and compassion toward all people.

The Lengths to Which One Will Go For a Cat

He sent his own Son in a human body like ours.
I Timothy 3:16 (TLB)

It's amazing what one will do for someone he loves. And it's amazing what one will do for a cat!

Although I live alone, and sleep alone—no, I don't live alone and sleep alone! I live and sleep with a cat! Anyway, I sleep on the right side of the bed, probably because that side's closer to the window and I can get the soft summer breezes that float in through the screen, even on the hottest of nights. Since I sleep on the right side of the bed, it's logical that I get in and out of bed on that side, too. Right? Wrong! I climb in and out from the left side, but there's a method in my madness.

First of all, I'm a night owl; and by walking stealthily on the left side of the bedroom, I don't have to worry about awakening my landlord and his wife whose bedroom is directly beneath mine, especially as they retire several hours before I do. The floor boards in an older house have a tendency to creak and groan, you know. Perhaps more important is the fact that using the left side of the bed affords a more direct path to the bathroom in the middle of the night!

What does all that have to do with Fluffy? Sometimes Fluffy decides she is going to sleep on the left side of the bed, too, curled up against my back. I can't just roll on top of her when I have the urge to scratch in my kitty litter, so what do I do? I can't just pick her up and move her—why, that would be unthinkable! So how do I manage? I wiggle and "scootch" and "scootch" and wiggle until I get past her warm little body and can continue my nightly trek to the bathroom!

At such times I shake my head in disbelief and groggily mutter to myself, *What lengths one will go to for a cat!* Then a second, but more sobering thought, comes to mind, *And what lengths God has gone to for mankind!*

Thank You, Jesus, for taking on Yourself a human body like mine just to provide the wonderful plan of Redemption for me. And thank You, Father, for sending Your Son to this world, God Himself come in the flesh. What lengths You have gone to to save sinful man. With all of my heart I thank You for Your boundless, unspeakable love.

The Longsuffering of Patience

Be patient with each other, making allowance for each other's faults because of your love.
Ephesians 4:2 (TLB)

I learned the correct way to spell "longsuffering" from a Bible teacher at summer camp many years ago: l-o-o-o-o-o-o-o-o-o-o-o-ngsuffering with as many "o's" as needed to cover your particular situation. Neat, huh?

Without bragging, I can truthfully say that's the kind of longsuffering I have with Fluffy—with one exception, that is. That's when she jumps on my lap and sticks her little pink nose in my food. You see, I like to eat while reclining in my La-Z-Boy. Strange as it may seem, that's when I get my daily exercise! When she thinks I have food, she immediately plops herself on my lap and tries to ferret out what I am eating. I twist to the right carefully lifting my bowl of soup above her head. Then I twist to the left stretching my arms as far as I can in an effort to get the soup past her inquisitive nose. But when she climbs on the phone stand, my arms can no longer reach past her hungry little mouth. I do a push-up with the soup bowl next. I know it doesn't come close to equaling a 25- or 50-lb. weight, but surely keeping the soup from spilling on my head is an accomplishment. Undaunted, Fluffy jumps on the back of the recliner.

"Fluffy," I scold in exasperation, "I don't stick my nose in your food. Now return the favor and get out of here." And with a gentle but unceremonious shove, I push her off my lap! I don't think I get beyond two or three of those "o's" in spelling longsuffering!

She sulks, of course, even though she knows I'll give her my empty dish to clean ("Yuk," I hear someone say!); but at least I can finish my meal in peace. Does she ever learn? No! A thousand times No!

Father, I know I'll never learn all the lessons You want me to. But I thank You that You never push me away in disgust, but with the utmost patience and longsuffering will keep working on me to make me what I ought to be—a miniature replica of Your very own self. May I, in turn, show the same love and patience toward my fellow men, making allowance for their faults even as I want them and You to do for me.

The Older She Gets

I will follow you no matter where you go.
Matthew 8:19 (TLB)

"Isn't it hard living alone?" well-meaning friends often ask me. To the contrary, I prefer to live by myself. Why? Because I enjoy privacy. I also enjoy intelligent company—that's why I talk to myself so much!

Did I just say I enjoyed privacy? What privacy? There's no such thing as privacy so long as Fluffy's around, especially as she gets older!

Today's a prime example. I slept late as I seemed to have a touch of the flu bug that's been making the rounds lately. She stayed in bed with me until the clock—well, never mind what the clock said! When I groggily stumbled to the bathroom to wash the sleep from my eyes, she was right behind me, winding around my legs whenever she could. I don't know what keeps me from stumbling over her and breaking some bones—both hers and mine! As I stopped in the kitchen to start my breakfast, she stopped, too, and looked up at me pleadingly for hers. Back in the bedroom, I wasted no time in donning a blouse and jumping into my culottes before making the bed—all of which I was trying to accomplish before she finished her breakfast. No such luck! I had to pause in the midst of putting the bedspread and throw pillows in place as she bounded onto the bed and slowly padded across it before jumping onto the night stand to peer out the window for her morning inspection of the back yard.

Devotions came next; and as usual, she made herself at home on my lap without so much as a "by-your-leave." When I turned on the computer and began writing, she curled up at my feet. She wasn't too happy when I made her go outdoors a few hours later while I went to the post office. I hoped she would "get lost" somewhere on our quarter-acre plot and enjoy the sunshine for a bit. Nothing doing. I was reclining in my La-Z-Boy (I think I should really call it "La-Z-Girl.") not five minutes later, reading my mail and the newspaper, when she clamored up on my lap once more—mainly to check out the slice of toast I was nibbling on, I'm sure!

Since I'm a light sleeper, I often go from the bed to the davenport in the middle of the night—several times over, I might add. Who's right behind me? Three guesses and the first two don't count! The older she gets, the worse she is with this type of conduct. But I wouldn't have it any other way!

I don't know whether Bill Gaither would approve or not, but I have my own version of his gospel song, "The Longer I Serve Him." It goes, "The longer I have her, the sweeter she grows." And when Fluffy answers with the next refrain, "The more that I love her, more love she bestows," I know I'd willingly give up my privacy any day to hear her soft, musical purr.

Father, truly You do grow sweeter as the days go by and I learn to love You more and more. May my love for You increase on a daily basis as I allow You to control every area of my life.

'Til The Storm Passes By'

O Lord, you are a refuge from the storm.
Isaiah 25:4 (TLB)

I'll bet Mosie Lister, author of " 'Til the Storm Passes By," had a cat! Isn't it logical to think that's where he got the inspiration for that wonderful hymn of assurance? She probably slept on the foot of his bed, too, as Fluffy does. (I use "she" since that's what Fluffy is. To my way of thinking, all cats are "she's" except for a few toms! Am I smart, or what?)

Lightning doesn't bother Fluffy. She'll jump on the night stand next to my bed and gaze out the window even when forked flashes have me burrowing under the covers. Once the thunder begins its noisy serenade, however, rapidly crescendoing among the creaking old oaks and evergreens of our woodsy backyard, she frantically dives under the bed, slithers across the floor, belly dragging the carpet, and finds shelter in the back of my closet.

How I long to tuck her under the blanket with me, cuddle her safely in the crook of my elbow and let her bury her head under my arm. But no amount of coaxing has ever persuaded her to leave the relative safety of her self-imposed sanctuary. My arthritis, you understand, precludes my crawling under the bed and into the closet with her. And there she stays until the storm has unleashed its fury and, as the song says, "the thunder sounds no more."

Eventually, she's learned, the storm passes by. It always does!

Oh, Lord, save me from relying on myself for protection in times of trouble, for I know that You long to hide me in the hollow of Your hand. May I always fly to You for shelter when the storms of life unleash their fury, remembering to call upon You to "Hold me fast 'til the storm passes by."

Cat Trivia

RESOLUTIONS ADOPTED BY THE LOCAL NEIGHBORHOOD KAT KONKLAVE

RESOLVED, cats should drive their humans bonkers.

RESOLVED, cats should whine and pace the floor to let their humans know they are unhappy.

RESOLVED, cats should do whatever they want to do whenever they want to do it no matter what their humans think about it.

RESOLVED, cats should appear to love it when their humans whisper secrets to them.

RESOLVED, cats need never worry about suffering from insomnia.

RESOLVED, cats should seldom listen to their humans.

RESOLVED, cats should leave their hair everywhere so their humans know they were there.

RESOLVED, cats should behave in a totally unpredictable manner.

RESOLVED, cats are permitted to be moody.

RESOLVED, cats should expect their humans to cater to their every whim.

RESOLVED, cats should try to engage their humans in play whenever said humans are reading a newspaper.

Trapped

...(H)e rescues you from every trap.
Psalm 91:3 (TLB)

Returning from the post office, I unceremoniously threw myself down on my favorite chair to see what Uncle Sam had delivered to me that day and gave a sigh of expectancy. That sigh alerted Fluffy I was home (I had been gone only fifteen minutes!), and she meowed for my attention. That was unusual in itself, for she hardly ever meows. I looked all around. No Fluffy. The sound of her continued cries told me she was in trouble.

Dashing downstairs at top speed, I searched and called, called and searched. The howls intensified, but no Fluffy appeared. I was alone on the hilltop that day and had no one to help me in my frantic endeavors to locate her. In a state of near panic, I rushed inside again and soon determined that her plaintive cries were coming from between the inside and outside walls of my living room! Apparently she had been chasing chipmunks under the third-floor eaves—a pastime she thoroughly enjoyed—and had fallen into the narrow space between the two walls. Not knowing that the floor extended across both walls, I envisioned her falling even further—to the first floor; worse yet, to the basement! I knew there was no way she could make it out of her trap because a former owner had had her front paws declawed.

I telephoned the volunteer fire department; no one was on duty! By this time I don't know who was crying harder—Fluffy or me! How soon would my landlord and his wife be home? And why did the neighbors decide to go away, too?

Between my sobs, I continued talking to Fluffy, coaxing and begging her to try harder to climb out. When everything was deathly silent for a few moments, I was sure she had, indeed, fallen the rest of the way to the basement! Suddenly I heard such an unearthly racket that I wondered if she was trying to claw a hole through the wall. Then silence again, except for my muffled sobs.

Suddenly, to my utter astonishment, I saw the most beautiful sight I've ever laid eyes on—a dirty, dingy orange and white blob literally throwing herself down in total exhaustion on the living room rug! She loved me enough to answer my call even though it took every ounce of her feline strength.

I'll never figure out how she ever climbed the studs with no front claws! What I do know, though, is that all entries to the third-floor attic space were covered with wire meshing before she got out in the front hallway again. Her years of playing in the dirt attic on the third floor were over!

Lord Jesus, thank You for loving me so much that You willingly answered my call for help when I was at the end of my own strength. Thank You for saving me though it took not only all Your strength, but also Your very life itself on the cruel cross of Calvary. What love! What marvelous love!

Tricked

"Can anything good come from there?"
John 1:46 (TLB)

That's the same question Fluffy asks every time she goes to the vet! When we return home, this is followed by a second, and similar, question: "Can anything good come from taking that medicine?"

For a few years, Fluffy's diet was dry cat food only—no canned food allowed except on holidays such as Thanksgiving and Christmas. When the vet would allow me the choice of giving her any necessary medication in tablet or liquid form, I knew better than to try a pill. No way would I be able to get her to swallow it. She knew how to use those sharp teeth to her advantage, and I wasn't about to put myself at her mercy twice a day. So inevitably I asked for liquid medicine.

Now no cat in its right mind would eat dry food with an antibiotic dribbled on it whether for looks or for added incentive. So off to the super market I'd go and load my cart with the most expensive and fancy canned cat food on the shelves! I justified my extravagance by reasoning that Fluffy deserved the best since she was sick. After all, this was the least I could do, and it might appease her wrath toward me for taking her to the vet in the first place.

I smirked to myself at how easy it was to get her to take her medicine once it was mixed with canned food. She never did discover how I tricked her, not just for one or two meals, or even one or two days, but for ten consecutive days at a time! It worked every time!

Oh, yes, there was the subsequent agony of weaning her off the canned food—but that's a different story! Yes, good can come from taking medicine, even for cats!

Father, often times when I encounter difficulties and hardships in my life, I'm tempted to complain and wonder why. Sorrow and grief enter my life and I don't understand it. Sometimes my plans fail, disappointments come, and I'm heavy-hearted and feel alone. Nevertheless, Lord, I know You're guiding me in paths that will increase my spiritual strength. I renew my vows before You that by Your grace and Your help, I'll follow You knowing, and trusting that You will bring good out of every situation in my life.

Unclaimed Blessing

I have learned, in whatsoever state I am,
therewith to be content.
Philippians 4:11 (KJV)

No longer can I boast of being an "unclaimed blessing." Nor can I lay claim to being sweet sixteen and never been kissed! Fluffy has seen to it that both statements are false—but then, I really don't mind, for I'm convinced I have a better life than some of my married friends.

It goes without saying that Fluffy and I claim each other as the #1 blessing in our lives—next to the Lord, that is. No kisses could be sweeter than those we exchange daily! We're constantly assured of our mutual love as we whisper sweet nothings in each other's ears every now and then. And oh, the love songs we sing, making up the lyrics as we go. Never mind they don't always rhyme!

At night I have someone to sleep with, a soft, cuddly someone who never "hogs" the blankets and never complains that the temperature's too hot or too cold.

At chow time I never have to listen to what wonderful meals her mother used to make. And I don't live in fear lest she bring unannounced guests for dinner.

She never chides me for not being able to find her clean socks or for neglecting to sew a button on her shirt. If I don't get the cleaning done promptly, she doesn't mind in the least. In fact, she likes to find afghans draped across the furniture, for they make such cozy places to snuggle for naps now and then.

In the mornings it doesn't bother her to see me without makeup or with my hair in curlers. And she pays absolutely no attention if I run around the apartment in my housecoat and bedroom slippers all day. She doesn't feel slighted if I bury my face in the newspaper with my morning coffee. She quietly jumps on my lap, slips under the paper, and curls up for a siesta.

When it comes to finances, she lets me handle the money and doesn't berate me for not paying the bills on time; and she never accuses me of being a spendthrift. What more could one desire in a companion?

Well-meaning friends sometimes query, "Don't you get lonely living alone?"

"I don't live alone," I reply with a condescending smile. "I have the Lord—and Fluffy!"

Thank You, Father, for the gift of singleness that so fits my personality. Truly You know what each of us needs in the area of companionship and will faithfully lead us in that direction so long as we keep our trust in You. Thank You, too, for the contentment that comes with being in the center of Your will in all circumstances, including matrimonial affairs.

Unconditional Love

I have loved thee with an everlasting love.
Jeremiah 31:3 (KJV)

Fluffy has her own inimitable ways of begging for attention. Her main ploy is to wait until I'm rushing around the house doing who-knows-what and run in front of me, lie down on the floor and curl herself into a crescent shape too cute to resist. Usually I stop whatever I'm doing and humor her. Other times I just ignore her. Undaunted, she jumps to her feet, runs past me and once again winds herself into that adorable little ball, paws upstretched so beseechingly.

As difficult as it is, there are times when my busy schedule forces me to ignore her completely. Not to be put off that easily, she continues her demanding antics not in the least discouraged by my brush-offs. Should I eventually sit down, without an invitation she jumps on my lap with a self-satisfied smirk on her upturned kitty face that says as plainly as words, "I knew I'd win if I kept on loving you even though you ignored me."

What a picture of God's unconditional love for you and me! And it's so comforting to know that He never ignores me the way I sometimes ignore Fluffy.

Heavenly Father, words are inadequate to thank You for loving me with an unconditional, everlasting love. No matter what I do nor where I go, You are there loving me still, for You've promised never to leave me or forsake me. Thank You! Thank You! Thank You!

Under His Wings

All humanity takes refuge in the shadow of your wings.
Psalm 36:7 (TLB)

I haven't sprouted wings, yet, that I'm aware of, but no one has informed Fluffy of that disappointing fact. Never is she more contented than when she can jump on my lap and bury her cold little nose under my arm. Perhaps in her little "kitty mind" she thinks of my arms as wings. At least I'd like to think it's more than my vanilla-scented perfume that attracts her. On those occasions her internal "buzz saw" works overtime as her front paws jog in place fast and furiously. I think of a dear friend of mine who would never allow her kittens to "knead" on anyone or even each other once they were weaned. Apparently I'm the spineless mother who gives in to all her baby's whims; but I've never had the heart to deny what gives my little one so much pleasure! After all, I reason, it's not as though she were hurting someone.

She does the same thing when we go to bed at night. Only then she nudges her way under the bed clothes before she curls up in the crook of my arm and "does her thing." Perchance I should take a midafternoon nap, she jumps on my chest and buries her head in the nape of my neck before pawing in contentment.

I have no trouble empathizing with Fluffy. For I also like to cuddle when the alarm sounds its raucous early-morning wake-up call. Although I don't have another person to snuggle up to—sorry, girls, not interested—or a pair of wings to hide beneath, I do pound a few soft spots into my pillow and curl a little deeper under the cozy blankets for a last-minute snooze which, more often than not, turns into an hour or more! After all, I am retired, and for years have looked forward to "sleeping in" as long as I wanted. Besides, when I'm lying snug and warm in a comfortable bed, I have no aches and pains— not even my arthritis bothers me! Nor do I have to make decisions about what I'm going to do the rest of the day or concern myself with what might happen or what the weather's like, etc.!

So, do your thing, Fluffy, do your thing! I love it when you do.

Father, thank You for the privilege of hiding beneath the shadow of Your wings; for it is there, when earth has no balm for my healing, that I find comfort and rest.

Understanding Cat Language

My words are plain and clear to anyone with half a mind.
Prov. 8:9 (TLB)

I had just settled down in my easy chair in the hopes of "losing myself" in the depths of a most interesting book when the phone startled me with its garrulous b-r-r-r-ing.

"Just wanted you to know," said my landlady who lives downstairs, "that I sent Fluffy inside and closed your back door." Because a stranger had pulled in the drive and knocked on their door, she knew I'd want "my baby" in the safety of the house. "Fluffy wasn't too happy about being sent upstairs," added Willie, "and told me so."

I heard, rather than saw, Fluffy as she came immediately to my chair and rudely interrupted our conversation. In fact, she "talked" nonstop from the moment she entered the kitchen door, continuing her complaint as she crossed the kitchen and came in to the living room where I was still on the phone.

"Here she is, now," I laughed, "telling me all about it."

I really can't recall when and how I learned to understand cat language. But I know, however, that it's a priority for cat owners!

Why, just today I was attending an all-day conference at church. Fluffy was outdoors when I left, and I didn't have time to hunt for her. (My toes were peeking out my toeless shoes and I really didn't want to get them wet in the early morning dew.) Ben, my landlord, said he'd look out for her until I got back around 3:00 or 3:30 in the afternoon.

Well, it was 4:00 o'clock before I finally got home, and Fluffy wasn't there to greet me! I walked around the house to her favorite haunt under the side porch, and sure enough, there she was! We detoured to our back door via Ben and Willie's kitchen, and as soon as Fluffy saw Ben, she began "spouting off" at him. (You see, Ben, too, has learned cat language. In fact, he advocates telling pets about your plans in advance and explaining in detail what's going on.)

Turning to me he explained, "She was in the house with me all afternoon until I told her what time you'd be home," he said. "Then she wanted out to meet you, but you were late. I've already apologized to her twice," he lamented, shaking his head, "and she's not getting another apology no matter how much she scolds!"

These are not isolated instances. Time and again Fluffy will go downstairs and complain to Ben about me. Other times she'll come upstairs and tell me what's going on out in the yard. While we may not understand, in all honesty, exactly what she's saying, it's very obvious that she is attempting to relate some important happening in her little cat life; for as Ben and I check with each other later, we usually learn that something or other, indeed, has occurred!

To us, her words are plain and clear to anyone with half a mind! And I'm sure Fluffy must think that's all the mind Ben and I have at times!

Now, what about God and me?

Heavenly Father, although I may not always be able to phrase my thoughts and petitions to You in flowery language and beautiful rhetoric, I thank You because You know and understand exactly what I'm trying to say. Thank You for the wisdom You give, and thank You for making Your words plain and clear to even me.

Wave the Banner Proudly

The Lord is my banner.
Exodus 17:15 (Amp)

Jehovah-Nissi—the Lord is my flag, my banner.

Fluffy has her own flag, her own banner—namely, her tail which she proudly waves for all to see! Often it's the only clue I have as to her whereabouts when she is exploring whatever it is that cats hunt for in vacant lots. Even when she's crouched in the deep grass stalking prey which she'll probably never catch, she waves that banner, albeit on a horizontal plane. Ben, my landlord, claims that an upright tail, however, is an indication she's feeling good. Following her infrequent bouts of ill health, he always watches for that perpendicular sign of physical fitness which assures us that once again she has made a full recovery and is embarking on another one of her nine lives.

There's just one drawback to that slowly waving pennant she so proudly displays: it serves as a first-class temptation to me, for I love the feel of that soft cylindrical tail weaving through my fingers. Sometimes she'll let me stroke it three or four times before switching it out of my reach and tucking it around her body. Other times she pulls away. Now can I help it, I ask you, if Fluffy walks off when her tail is still in my hand? Then the hissing and spitting begin as she has the gall to accuse me of actually pulling it!

Life just isn't fair! If she doesn't want to be teased, then she need not flaunt her banner in my face!

Thank You, Father, because Your banner over me is love. Help me to wave that standard proudly before those of my fellow men who do not know about Your faithfulness, Your grace, and Your mercy. Through my love to them, placed in my heart by You, may they, too, be introduced to a personal relationship with the God of the universe that will cause them, in turn, to unfurl their own banner of love so that the entire world will see Your children marching in unity under the leadership of Jehovah-Nissi.

What a Change

...(W)e. . .are changed. . .from glory to glory.
II Corinthians 3:18 (KJV)

For several years Fluffy drained my already-tight budget to the breaking point by begging for kitty treats. Fortunately I'm a coupon clipper, and I also harassed my catless friends to save their "cat coupons" for me. I would never have made ends meet otherwise.

When one friend showed me how he had trained both his cats to reach their paws into a bag of treats and get their own juicy morsels, I decided I'd do the same thing. After all, as I've boasted before, Fluffy is smart, even though you may think I'm somewhat prejudiced! But Fluffy wouldn't be trained. She was as determined as I was—and not only that, she won out!

However, that's not the end of the story. She has refused to eat kitty treats for me ever since! I gave umpteen cans and bags of Pounce and Whisker Lickin' Good's to my friend and then turned green with envy as I watched his cats devour their good fortune with relish! And know what else? Fluffy still eats kitty treats for Ben and Willie, my landlord and his wife—she just won't eat them for me! Is she stubborn, or what? (An inherited trait from her mother's side of the family, I suppose!)

I can almost hear her sing her version of an old Sunday School chorus, "The things I used to eat, don't eat them any more; there's a great change since I have taken my stand."

Thank You, Father, for the great and marvelous change there's been in my life since I gave my heart to You. And thank You, too, because You are continually changing me from glory to glory.

Who's First?

...(G)ive him first place in your life.
Matthew 6:33 (TLB)

Fluffy's an excellent alarm clock. She knows that because I'm a night owl, I like to sleep late in the mornings—in fact, early morning is when I do my best sleeping. But just let nine—well, never mind exactly what time it is, we'll simply say when it's time for me to wake up, she trots to the head of the bed and sings her version of a little ditty my father used to sing:

Oh, it's nice to get up in the morning,
when the sun begins to shine,
At three or four or five o'clock in the good,
old summertime.
But when the snow begins to fall,
and it's cloudy overhead,
Oh, it's nice to get up in the morning,
but it's nicer to stay in bed.

I don't know if that was one of Father's original songs or not. Be that as it may, my favorite part of the verse has always been those last seven words of the final line!

Then one day I had a guilt attack as a nasty little voice whispered in my ear, "If you're such a good Christian, don't you think your waking thoughts should be on the Lord instead of Fluffy?"

Later, a similar voice whispered in my other ear, "What kind of a Christian are you, anyway? You've made your bed, dressed, eaten your breakfast, and fed the cat—all before you've had devotions. Don't you think the Lord should come first?"

By that time my guilt was compounded by condemnation. All day long the bombardment continued. "You spend more time with Fluffy than with the Lord," accused my conscience. "You're more concerned about your cat than about spiritual things," my mind censured me. "Fluffy's more important to you than the Lord." On and on it went throughout the day.

Suddenly I realized the source of all those negative thoughts as the Holy Spirit quietly reminded me that if we first draw nigh to God, we are in a position to resist the devil. "Lord," I prayed, much like Peter, "You know my heart, and You know I love You best of all." Peace reigned within once again and I was reminded that guilt and condemnation are altogether different from conviction, and are not from the Lord.

Thank You, Father, for Your Word that assures me You did not send Your Son into this world to bring condemnation, but life, eternal life. Help me always to be able to distinguish between the conviction of the Holy Spirit and the guilt and condemnation that comes from the enemy of my soul. And thank You because You know the very thoughts and intents of my heart, and You know that You're first in my life. I love You more than anyone or anything on earth—even Fluffy.

Worry Wart

In all you do, I want you to be free from worry.
I Corinthians 7:32 (TLB)

I can only ascertain what might be going through Fluffy's little kitty mind by her behavior. Her actions seldom leave room for doubt.

During times of recuperation after some slight illness, she doesn't want me out of her sight. She was hospitalized only once, but wouldn't even go outdoors without me when she returned home. In fact, she refused to go out on the front porch unless I went, too. Leaving the screen door open and assuring her I was sitting in my La-Z-Boy just around the corner did nothing to alleviate her fears that she might be abandoned again if she didn't keep her eyes on me. (If only I had sense enough to keep my eyes on the Lord like that!)

My vacation time and occasional short trips aren't quite such a trauma for her, for she then stays with Ben and Willie, my landlord and his wife who live downstairs. She's down there a good share of the time, anyway, when I'm home, so she doesn't feel forsaken when I do disappear for a few days. Of course, she disdainfully gives me the cold shoulder for a few minutes when I return, just to register her displeasure, but it's obvious she doesn't worry that I may never come home again.

Another period of her life when Fluffy exhibited traits of anxiety was one summer when the neighbors' cats would visit us, uninvited, every now and then. On each occasion she cautiously looked out the kitchen door and all around the back attic before venturing outside. When she finally made it to the top of the stairs, she cocked her head and looked around the corner to see if any of her self-declared kitty enemies were coming up the steps. Once downstairs, she stood in the open door and critically surveyed the outside world before venturing further. Anxiety, personified!

Do cats worry? I don't rightly know—but I do know that people worry! You don't suppose Fluffy inherited her trait of worrying from her owner, do you? Maybe I'd better teach her that old Sunday School chorus that asks, "Why worry, when you can pray?"

Thank You, Lord, for the privilege of casting all my care upon You because You want Your children to be free from worry and anxiety. You know what my needs are and have promised to supply those needs according to Your riches in glory. And I praise You because those riches are endless and because all that You have is available to me.

Wrestling Match

For we are not fighting against people made of flesh and blood, but. . . against huge numbers of wicked spirits in the spirit world.
Ephesians 6:12 (TLB)

Fluffy has one of the nicest vets—at least I think so. He's friendly; he's kind; he's gentle; and he's caring. In fact, the day after Fluffy has been treated for some unexpected ailment, he always has his office call me to inquire regarding her progress. Now, I ask you, just how many vets do that?

Fluffy, on the other hand, thinks I'm opinionated. She has absolutely no use for her doctor. She fights me when I put her into her cat carrier for the anticipated trip. Then she refuses to get out of the carrier when I place her on the examining table. Once she's been weighed, had her temperature taken, received her shot and any other medication she might need, however, she's more than willing to scramble inside the safety of that cat carrier without any urging from me. Why can't she be that co-operative at home about the forthcoming trip?

The one thing I can't figure out, though, is how she knows whom to hiss at when getting a shot. I'm the person holding her down so that she can't bite or scratch the vet, although on one occasion she somehow managed to sink her sharp teeth into his hand; but she doesn't hiss at me. She turns her head in his direction, as much as she possibly can, that is, glares into his eyes, and directs several ugly, nasty hisses in his direction, even though I've explained to her that she'll feel better after the shot and that he's doing it for her own good. (I heard that same explanation a few times myself, as a child—just before parental discipline was administered!)

Take heed, all you cat lovers. Like Fluffy, we need to know whom to hiss at in the spiritual realm. It's definitely not people!

Help me remember, Father, that the enemies I need to fight against are not flesh and blood people (although it often appears that way) but rather wicked spirits that use human beings through which to exert their evil influence and plans, often unknowingly to the individuals themselves. May my warfare always be directed toward those perverse spirits and not toward my fellowmen.

You're Home at Last

...(T)hen we will be at home with the Lord.
II Corinthians 5:8 (TLB)

I've always wanted a cat that would ride in the car, sit on the back of my seat, and survey the passing landscape as we leisurely drive through verdant countryside. I could envision such a furry companion also curling into a ball in the rear window and whiling away the hours on long trips. How I envy one acquaintance who enjoys the company of her cat on round trips between Florida and New York. But Fluffy has disappointed me in that regard. You must understand, of course, that I love her anyway, and would never, but never consider parting with her just because of that one little fault!

Since driving to and from the vet, a short trip of five miles, is such a futile exercise in patience on my part, whenever we make the infrequent jaunts, I need a good supply of nerve pills on hand—not for Fluffy, but for me!

On the homeward journey I breathe a sigh of relief when I can view the friendly blinker light in the center of our small town as it flashes its welcoming beam of encouragement; for

I know that once we reach that landmark, Fluffy will quiet down immediately as we make a left-hand turn and ascend the short hill leading to our street. Two more quick turns and Fluffy is finally free to roam the familiar territory she calls home.

Somehow that blinker light at the bottom of the hill is a signal to Fluffy that the end of her frustrating journey is at hand, and I can almost hear her singing her kitty version of an old Gospel song, "Going home, I'm going home. . .Praise God, I'm going home!"

Father, I, too, am anticipating the time when I can go "home" to be with You, away from all trouble and strife forevermore, for truly there will then be nothing to hold me here on this earth any longer. Thank You for the mansion You've prepared for me. Have the angels keep it ready. May my soul be spotless, for very soon the journey will end, and I'll be heading "home at last!"

You're Protected

You hem me in—behind and before.
Psalm 139:5 (NIV)

"Moving Day" was finally over, and that large, rambling "home place" overlooking the surrounding area began to fade into just a fond memory,

No longer was Fluffy "Queen of the Hill." No longer could she roam the countryside at will. The new home one hundred miles away drastically limited her outside gambols because the neighboring felines on both sides of the house were less than friendly to a strange pussy cat encroaching on their territory. Within a week or two, however, a lovely chain link fence, five feet tall, appeared in the back yard; and once again she was free to wander outdoors—within the confines of the fence, that is!

Now wouldn't you think that 800 square feet of space should be enough to keep any cat happy and content? Not Fluffy! She seized every possible opportunity to sneak up behind me on her velvety pink paws and slip out the gate whenever I went to the garden or the shed further back on the lot. Or she would hide behind the many interesting storage boxes in the attached garage, patiently waiting for the overhead garage doors to open, then spring to freedom like a jack-in-the-box. How careful I had to be, for "Arthur-Itis" now prevented me from moving fast enough to catch her.

I tried my best to explain to Fluffy that I was restricting her outdoor life for her safety and protection because I loved her. But somehow, she never seemed to believe me! Not even when I gently scolded her, "Fluffy, cats are supposed to be smart—smarter than dogs. But sometimes I think you don't even have the brains you were born with!"

Then I wonder, "Do I?"

Heavenly Father, may I always remember that it's because of Your great love for me that You set a hedge of protection around me. May I not be impatient to break through this boundary, for I know that in my own strength I cannot cope with the dangers and evils that are apt to befall me when I step outside of Your precious will. Your limitations are my protection.

You're Safe in My Arms

(U)nderneath are the everlasting arms.
Deuteronomy 33:27 (KJV)

The day eventually came when arthritis prevented Fluffy's human companion, namely me, from climbing the stairs to our second-floor apartment. That sad turn of events necessitated a move of one hundred miles to a one-story house next door to a close friend. Of course, moving to a much smaller dwelling meant we had to dispose of many items. What fun Fluffy had in "nosing" around through piles and boxes of articles accumulated throughout my 38 years of living in the same place! There were lots and lots of exciting "what-cha-ma-call-its" for her to check out since I have always been a packrat! And how she loved to jump inside the boxes as I packed those items we felt we just HAD to keep.

Eventually everything was either disposed of or loaded into the moving van, and the apartment was empty. By that time Fluffy realized that something strange was going on as she prowled restlessly from one room to another trying to find a familiar object of some kind. But all she could find was her owner's overnight bag with a few last-minute items for our final night's stay in what had been her home for the past ten years!

Fluffy has always resisted riding in a car, and now my one concern was how I could possibly drive one hundred miles while listening to her vociferous caterwauling with every rotation of the tires. Nor did I want to subject her to the trauma of a lengthy ride.

Then a retired couple from church offered their services. The husband drove their car for the one-hundred-mile jaunt while the wife drove mine. After wrapping "my baby" in a blanket, I sat in the passenger seat of my own car and held Fluffy on my lap for the entire journey. Apparently she felt safe and protected with my familiar arms cradling her, for she gave only a couple faint meows during the two-hour trip.

But then, don't we all feel safe when surrounded by the arms of those we love?

Father, thank You for Your everlasting arms that are always underneath and round about me, offering me security in times of upheaval and protecting me from the dangers—both real and imagined–that I encounter in my journey from earth to heaven.

Epilogue

Since completing these devotional vignettes, and just seven months after moving to our new home, I have had to say a final farewell to Fluffy. The inevitable happened when she contracted a rapidly growing cancer, one that is usually peculiar to dogs. Although she lost an alarming amount of weight, she did not seem to be in pain. However, as she became unable to eat or use her litter box, I knew the time had come when the kindest thing to do was to release her from her sad plight and send her beyond those catnip gates to the "kitty heaven" mentioned in the Preface of this book—where she could peacefully roam the vast fields of clover.

Fluffy had adapted marvelously to her new home, and I do miss her. But Boogie, Woogie, and Penelope (yes, you read that right—three new kitties) now keep me company and enjoy Fluffy's toys and her newly-fenced-in back yard.

I trust you have enjoyed reading these memorials to Fluffy as much as I have enjoyed writing them. My prayer is that they have been a blessing and inspiration to one and all.

The Last Battle

Author Unknown

If it should be that I grow frail and weak
And pain should keep me from my sleep,
Then will you do what must be done,
For this—the last battle—can't be won.

You will be sad, I understand,
But don't let grief then stay your hand;
For on this day, more than the rest,
Your love and friendship must stand the test.

We've had so many happy years;
And though 'twill cause you bitter tears,
You wouldn't want me to suffer, so
When the time comes, please, let me go.

Take me to where my needs they'll tend,
Only, stay with me till the end
And hold me firm and speak to me
Until my eyes no longer see.

I know, in time, you will agree
This is a kindness you can do for me.
Although my tail its last has waved,
From pain and suffering, I've been saved.

Don't grieve that it must be you
Who has to decide this thing to do.
We've been so close—we two—these years,
Don't let your heart hold any tears.

Printed in the United States
963500004B